T0361144

Politics in the Dutch Economy

The economics of institutional interaction

BART SNELS
Faculty of Public Administration and Public Policy
University of Twente
Enschede, The Netherlands

Routledge
Taylor & Francis Group

LONDON AND NEW YORK

First published 1999 by Ashgate Publishing

Reissued 2018 by Routledge
2 Park Square, Milton Park, Abingdon, Oxon OX14 4RN
711 Third Avenue, New York, NY 10017, USA

Routledge is an imprint of the Taylor & Francis Group, an informa business

Publisher's Note
The publisher has gone to great lengths to ensure the quality of this reprint but points out that some imperfections in the original copies may be apparent.

Disclaimer
The publisher has made every effort to trace copyright holders and welcomes correspondence from those they have been unable to contact.

A Library of Congress record exists under LC control number: 99072242

ISBN 13: 978-1-138-33248-5 (hbk)
ISBN 13: 978-0-429-44659-7 (ebk)

Contents

List of Figures

List of Tables

Acknowledgements

This book is about political economic interaction in the Netherlands. In recent years the Dutch model has been attracting international attention. This book, an adaptation of my doctoral thesis, explains how political mechanisms work in the Dutch economy and how important it is to consider the institutional framework in which decisions about economic policies are made.

I started the research at Utrecht University in 1993. I was an AIO for three years, the Dutch equivalent to a PhD-student, when I decided to broaden my view by leaving the university to become a policy advisor for GreenLeft, a political party in the Dutch parliament. Working at the university was interesting, but I needed to take a closer look at how politics really works. However, working as an economist for a political party and writing a doctoral thesis about political economic interaction are two different things. During the week I thought about day to day politics; at weekends I worked at theoretical political economic models. I thank my teachers at Utrecht University, Jan Reijnders and Yoe Brenner, as well as my GreenLeft colleagues for supporting me in finishing this book.

Writing a book is a lonely activity, but not one that you accomplish alone. There have been many friends and colleagues who in one way or another influenced my work. It is impossible to thank everyone personally. However, during my years as an AIO I had the good luck of having a group of special friends. They deserve a special word of gratitude. Bert van den Brink, Brigitte Boon and Jolle Demmers, thanks!

I am grateful for all the support my parents have been giving me ever since I left my hometown to study economics at Tilburg University. My girlfriend Cécile Gorter knows how much I am indebted to her. Finally, I thank the University of Twente for the opportunity of returning to and finishing this book in an academic environment. I am very pleased with the combination of working for GreenLeft and having a part-time job as an assistant professor of economics at the faculty of Public Administration and Public Policy.

Introduction

The subject of this book is the interaction between politics and economics. Because there are so many scientific approaches to the study of political economic interaction or political economy, this statement does not clarify what the book is about. The best way to give the reader an idea about the content is to enumerate the three most prominent articles discussed in the book. These articles are Nordhaus (1975), Hibbs (1977a) and Scharpf (1987). In simple terms, the two main questions are: (i) does it make a difference for the economy whether the government is left-wing or right-wing?; and (ii) do governments manipulate economic policies to enhance their chances to be re-elected? The general question is whether, and if so how, electoral and ideological political motivations influence economic policies and affect the economy in a capitalist democracy. These are positive research questions. The aim is to study the actual interrelation between democratic political mechanisms and economic outcomes. Despite personal political preferences - economic research is never neutral - there are no normative intentions.

Although the term political economy originates from classical economists such as Smith, Ricardo and Mill, there are many modern schools of thought within the economic sciences, from traditional Marxists to modern neo-classicals and monetarists, also adhering to this term (see, for example, De Beus, 1987; Clark, 1991; Caporaso and Levine, 1992). Classical political economy was a social science combining politics and economics. It had a normative denotation because it 'not only described how the economic system actually worked, or could work, but also how, according to the assumptions of the author, it ought to be made, or allowed, to work' (Robbins, 1976: 1). With the development of neo-classical economics in the nineteenth century political considerations disappeared and two separate disciplines emerged: economics and political science. Only Marx, and later on Marxist economists, preserved the term political economy (Groenewegen, 1987). However, in the twentieth century dissatisfaction with this separation led to new approaches to political economy. Esping-Andersen, following Robbins (1976), claimed that the fundamental distinction between most variants of modern political economy and classical political economy is that modern political economy 'defines itself as a positive science and shies away from normative prescription' (Esping-Andersen, 1990: 12). In one way or another the aim of all approaches to modern political economy is to study the actual relation between democratic politics and its influence on, or interrelation with, the economy. This common aim seems to point to a similarity between all approaches, namely the distinction made, at least analytically, between the economic and political sphere. Although these spheres are not clearly distinguishable, there is a difference between political and economic objectives (prosperity versus justice), between institutional arenas (the market versus the government) and between actors (individuals versus the community). The study of political economy is aimed at analysing the interaction between the political and economic sphere. It is clear that the role and the functioning of the state are of central importance to all approaches to political economy (Clark, 1991).

There are also non-economic-scientists claiming to study political economic interaction, for example political and social scientists. In general, these scientists claim to take explicit account of the historical, institutional and social context in which political economic interaction is taking place. To give the reader an idea about the different ways of studying modern political economy the classification system of Hemerijck (1992, 1994b) is used. Hemerijck, following Maier (1987), distinguished between two approaches to modern political economy: the *economics of politics* approach, referring especially to public choice theory (the neo-classical variant of modern political economy), and the *politics of economics* approach. The distinction is made for the following reasons. The economics of politics is an economic approach to politics, analysing human action in the political sphere. With respect to methodology the economics of politics explicitly emphasizes rational behaviour and assumes that preferences are fixed, exogenously determined and revealed in individual behaviour. In short, the economics of politics uses neo-classical economic theory to analyse politics.

In contrast, the politics of economics does not analyse individual behaviour, but studies the influence of political or institutional structures on the economy. It is more interested in collective entities and uses a comparative methodology. In stressing the role of collective entities the politics of economics approach looks for power relations that can explain economic outcomes. Power considerations are therefore more important in this approach than rationality problems. The focus is on the social, institutional and sometimes historical differences between countries in order to explain differences in economic performance. This approach is applied mainly by social and political scientists.

This twofold classification system is rather broad. There are so many models and theories that it is hard to classify them into only two categories. Nevertheless, this classification system intuitively makes sense. In this book the differences between the political mechanisms of the economics of politics and the influence of the political and institutional structures of the politics of economics are of special importance. An eclectic point of view is taken by discussing such different theories of political economic interaction and attaching importance to the various contributions.

The subject matter of this book stems from a personal fascination with political factors playing a role in determining economic policy, especially the role of political parties. In chapter one the literature of political economic interaction models is surveyed. The works of Nordhaus (1975) and Hibbs (1977a) are examples of political economic interaction models in which, respectively, opportunistic and ideological motives of democratically elected politicians, or political parties, determine economic policies. As a matter of fact, political economic interaction models may be classified into two categories: *political business cycles* (Nordhaus) and *partisan cycles* (Hibbs). Although both types of models attempt to explain economic outcomes by political factors, the explanations (and implications) are different, and at times even contradictory. In political business cycle models all political parties have, once they obtained control of the government, the same objective, namely to stay in power. Therefore, the economic policy of one party hardly differs from another's. Parties manipulate the economy with the objective to maximize their votes. Distinct from the 'vote-maximizing' parties there are also partisan models in which political parties have different objectives. With these, economic policy changes when there is a change of government. Consequently, economic outcomes can (partially) be explained by changing governments.

Both types of models are mechanistic economic models. Especially Nordhaus's political business cycle model is a clear example of the economics of politics approach. Also surveyed in chapter one is the literature on institutional interaction. Beside the research on political economic interaction models, which focuses on politicians (political parties) and voters, there is also research on comparative political economy. This research, which may be classified as part of the politics of economics approach, claims to take account of the institutional 'playing-field' in which political economic interaction is taking place. It is necessary not to neglect the role of other players in the political economic game, such as labour movements and employers' organizations. The theories of the politics of economics or comparative political economics stress the importance of institutional structures in determining economic policies and outcomes. However, they tend to neglect the possibility of political actors making policy choices dependent on economic and political circumstances. The political economic interaction models are perhaps too mechanistic, but the theories of comparative political economics too much stress the influence of the institutional structure. Therefore, the model of Scharpf (1987, 1991) is presented. This model may be regarded to be a combination of the politics of economics and the economics of politics approaches. The political motivations determining economic policy in the models of the political business cycle and the partisan theory (electoral and ideological goals) are combined with the institutional factors of the politics of economics. According to Scharpf's model it is the economic and political circumstances which determine the way in which political actors make their policy choices. Thus, the model of Scharpf is presented as a theoretical reaction to both the mechanistic political economic interaction models and the structuralistic approach of comparative political economics.

In chapter one it is argued that the two approaches of this book are not mutually exclusive. It is recognized that many theories or models may (only) explain part of reality. In this chapter the macroeconomic assumptions of the various political economic theories are considered as well as the assumptions regarding the political aspects of these theories. It is explained that the varying conclusions and implications from the different theories stem from varying methodological assumptions. Most of the models are too mechanistic and too simple to deserve to be called a theory of political economic interaction. However, it may just be that the reality of political economic interaction is too complex for the formulation of general theories or laws. Perhaps social scientists should acknowledge that it may only be possible to identify simple mechanisms in varying social political realities, and should not try to find general laws (see Elster, 1989).

The objective of this book is to compare some theories of political economic interaction and to critically review them. This is done in two ways. First, the limitations of the mechanistic interaction models come into sight by discussing the literature and by comparing these models with comparative political economics. The various political economic models are discussed and criticized in the first chapter. Second, by testing these models for the Netherlands the empirical relevance of the models is investigated. This is done in subsequent chapters. Despite the possible limitations of these models, an empirical investigation may lead to indications of the way in which political factors affect the Dutch economy.

The Netherlands may be an interesting case for testing political economic interaction models. The Dutch economy is small and open and the government consists of a coalition of political parties. These are two factors that complicate the rather simple theories of the political business cycle and the partisan theory. If there is empirical evidence for political business cycles or partisan cycles reported in the literature, it is mainly for large, more or less two-party democracies. Because the Dutch economy is small and open, and because the Dutch political system comprises many political parties and coalition governments, it is an intriguing question whether mechanistic political economic models, such as the political business cycle and the partisan cycle, have empirical relevance for the Netherlands. In chapter two the partisan theory is tested empirically. An attempt is made to find an ideological influence in Dutch economic variables. Does ideology affect the Dutch economy? If so, are these effects in accordance with partisan theory?

In chapter three the political business cycle models are subjected to an empirical test. These models predict even more systematic patterns in economic variables than the partisan models. There is not much research on political business cycles in the Netherlands, because it is difficult to imagine how in the Dutch economy a coalition government would be able to manipulate economic policies in such a way that all the political parties taking part in the government would electorally take advantage from such manipulation. However, it therefore is a challenge to investigate whether there are such effects in the Netherlands.

It may be clear from the outset that the empirical relevance of these models is limited. Therefore, in chapter four a framework is developed, which is inspired by Scharpf's model, to analyse political economic interaction in the Netherlands in a somewhat less mechanistic manner. The objective of chapter four is to demonstrate that a descriptive framework presents a more accurate explanation of ideological and electoral factors playing a role in Dutch political economic interaction than the mechanistic models. Important in this chapter is the role of the institutionalized labour movement and the employers' organizations. These political actors are ignored in the political business cycle and partisan models. Especially in the Dutch model of policy-making, which in recent years has been attracting so much international attention, these political actors are too important to neglect.

The book ends with a summary and some concluding comments. The objective is to evaluate some theories of political economic interaction and to establish whether these theories have explanatory power for Dutch political economic interaction. Did the empirical investigations present some indications of how the Dutch economy is affected by ideological and electoral political goals? In the concluding chapter the various theories are summarized and some critical remarks are made about political and economic aspects that were ignored by the theories discussed in the earlier parts of the book.

1 Models of Political Economic Interaction

1.1 Introduction

There are two categories of political economic interaction models: *political business cycles* and *partisan cycles*. The first type of model tries to explain economic policy by the opportunism of politicians, whereas the second type of model stresses the ideological motives of politicians or political parties in formulating economic policy. This chapter reviews these kinds of models. The chapter focuses on the role of political parties in political economic interaction.

In section two the theory of the political business cycle is surveyed. The literature on political business cycles is vast. The discussion about their empirical relevance and theoretical construction is still in progress. There seems, however, to be a measure of consensus about the observation that politicians wish the economy to look good around election time. Therefore, the timing of elections may well be affecting economic policy, but it may not be as systematic as a pattern of political business cycles implies.

Section three reviews the partisan theory. Politicians are not only motivated by opportunistic electoral motives, but they have ideological goals as well. It, therefore, seems logical to assume that political parties have distinct partisan goals which influence economic policy of distinct partisan governments. The mechanistic partisan models, assuming a business cycle caused by varying ideological governments, are discussed in this section.

In section four it is argued that it is important to consider the institutional surroundings in which political economic interaction is taking place. Specific attention is given to the role of labour and employers' organizations. Corporatist structures and the partisan composition of governments are central themes in comparative political economics. This branch of research, which may be categorized as part of the politics of economics, is discussed in this section to comment on the mechanistic models of political economic interaction.

1.2 The Political Business Cycle

The Kaleckian Political Business Cycle

In 1943 Kalecki wrote about the political business cycle in his famous article 'Political aspects of full employment' (Kalecki, 1971). The Keynesian revolution had just started with Keynes's 'General Theory' published in 1936 (Keynes, 1973). At that time there was a discussion in the economic sciences about the possibility of achieving and maintaining full employment. The Keynesian revolution advanced the idea that full employment could be reached and maintained by public spending and monetary policy. Politics in early Keynesianism meant that politicians had to be convinced by economists to execute a demand management policy. The task of economists was to calculate the necessary policies. The Dutch economist Tinbergen is an important example of an economist who thought along Keynesian lines. According to Tinbergen, economists would calculate what has to be done and politicians would execute calculated, fine-tuned policies. By coordinated economic policies economic crises and structural unemployment would be prevented (Tinbergen, 1970; see also Keech, 1995).

Kalecki, however, pointed out that the problem of unemployment is not only an economic problem, but that political realities have to be taken into account as well. In his view there are different reasons why 'big business' dislikes the maintenance of full employment by government spending: '(i) the dislike of Government interference in the problem of employment as such; (ii) the dislike of the direction of Government spending (public investment and subsidising consumption); and (iii) dislike of the social and political changes resulting from the *maintenance* of full employment' (Kalecki, 1971: 139, italics in original). 'Their class instinct [of the business leaders] tells them that lasting full employment is unsound from their point of view and that unemployment is an integral part of the normal capitalist system' (Kalecki, 1971: 141). So, whenever the government succeeds in achieving full employment, business leaders will try to convince the government to cut the budget deficit. A slump will follow and the government has again to expand its spending to bring down unemployment. Kalecki named this pattern the political business cycle: a business cycle caused by political motivations.

In 1975 (more than thirty years after the publication of Kalecki's article) the Marxist economists Boddy and Crotty used post World War II data to prove the existence of a Kaleckian political business cycle in the United States. They concluded 'on the basis of an examination of the data that the political-economic function of macropolicy in the short-run is not to pursue sustained full employment nor a steady, relaxed economy with a stable reserve army. Rather its function is to ensure that the alternating pressures for expansion and contracting emanating from the private sector result in that cyclical pattern most conducive to long-run profit maximization. *The goal of macropolicy is not to eliminate the cycle but to guide it in the interests of the capitalist class*' (Boddy and Crotty, 1975: 10, italics in original).[1]

The theoretical framework of Kalecki is Marxist for two reasons. Firstly, Kalecki (and Boddy and Crotty) perceived the character of the state as functionalist. The state collaborates with the capitalists in order to secure capitalist interests. Secondly, the theory is class based (see also Locksley, 1980). Following Borooah and Van der Ploeg (1983: 78), the Marxist view of politics is 'broad', meaning 'that the mechanism generating the cycles is class conflict based on conflict over the division of economic spoils, with the government aiding the capitalist class and organised labour constraining their ability to do so'. In other words, the government acts as one monolithic actor in the interest of the capitalists. Neither democratic political parties, with party-specific objectives, nor democratic politicians, with re-election goals, play a role in generating the political business cycle.

An exception in the Marxist tradition is Glombowski (1988, 1989, 1991), who developed a Marxist business cycle model consisting of a political sector and an economic sector.[2] The economic sector is based on a Goodwin profit squeeze cycle (see Goodwin, 1967). In the political sector there are two parties which, whenever in power, pursue different policies. The right-wing party eliminates state sector employment in order to bring down taxation (private employment is stimulated by this

---

[1] For the Dutch economy Wilke (1991b) noted that the study of Visser and Wijnhoven (1989), who interviewed politicians, employers and leaders of the labour movement, supports the theory of Kalecki. This study revealed that it was a political choice not to fight mass unemployment in the Netherlands in the 1980s. Especially employers demonstrated an aversion against full employment.

[2] For an elaboration of Marxist theory, modern political theory and the exception of the Glombowski model, see also Wilke (1991a: 85).

measure). The left-wing party does not want to wait for private employment to rise and takes action by programmes for state employment. The connections between the economic and political cycle result in a political economic cycle with alternating regimes. This strictly theoretical model is an example of the democratic class struggle. State power is the objective of a democratic struggle along class lines, and it depends on the voters which policy regime will prevail for a certain amount of time (at least until the next general election). In other words, democracy and the existence of political parties with different objectives determine whether the state acts in the interest of the capitalist class or in the interest of the working class. Distinct partisan goals are crucial for theories about partisan cycles. These theories are discussed in section three.

The Nordhaus Political Business Cycle

Kalecki's article may be regarded a starting-point for the study of the influence of democracy on the capitalist economy. Mainstream economists, like their Marxist colleagues, took an interest in the relation between democratic politics and developments in the economy. Instead of doing research on what policy the government should employ in order to solve a particular economic problem, the research question shifted to what governments actually do and how this is related to economic circumstances and vice versa. Since the 1950s mainstream public choice economists have been engaged in analysing politics by using the neo-classical toolbox (Buchanan, 1984). One of the pioneers who started this research on mainstream political economics was Downs.

Downs developed his influential model of politics and economics in his book *An Economic Theory of Democracy* (Downs, 1957). His main thesis was that political parties are vote-maximizers and are therefore similar to profit-maximizing firms. According to this theory there is no government that tries to maximize social welfare. Politicians have goals of their own, and one of those is to win elections to come to or to stay in power.[3] A politician in office will employ those policies he believes will gain the most votes. It is on the basis of this assumption about the behaviour of politicians that the modern models of political business

---

[3] See for ideas about political competition also Schumpeter (1976), and, very early, Hotelling (1929).

cycles are constructed. From 1975 on, a vast amount of literature has been written about models of political economic interaction. Nordhaus reintroduced the term political business cycle in 1975, although the interpretation of the term differs from what Kalecki meant by it.[4] Downsian vote-maximizing political parties induce in the Nordhaus-model the pattern of political business cycles. Nordhaus's main assumptions are: (i) political parties in power can manipulate the economy, or more precisely, can manipulate the Phillips curve; (ii) political parties are only interested in maximizing votes; (iii) voters are myopic, that is, they are only interested in the next election; and (iv) their votes depend on economic outcomes.

The political party that wins the election will first employ a deflationary policy to bring down inflation. Unemployment will rise as a consequence of such a policy. Then, towards the next election, unemployment will slowly fall and inflation will gradually rise until 'the purely myopic point', meaning that it is not sustainable in the long run (Nordhaus, 1975: 184). After the election again a deflationary policy will be undertaken to bring down inflation, but which causes unemployment.[5] According to Nordhaus this short-term (myopic) pattern of policy causes,

---

[4] See, however, Byung Hee Soh (1986) for a historical account on the use of the term political business cycle in the literature.

[5] Monetarism of the 1960s criticized the stable Keynesian trade-off between inflation and unemployment. According to monetarists, economic subjects take account of expected government policy, be it that expectations are adaptive (accommodating government policy takes some time). Producers foresee the inflationary consequences of an expansionary policy and adjust their prices; employees set their real wage demands on the basis of expectations about government policy and its inflationary consequences. Because expectations are adaptive, only in the short run a temporary rise in employment is possible. In the long run expansionary economic policy is ineffective, meaning that unemployment remains at the so-called natural rate (Friedman, 1976). A lasting unemployment rate below the natural rate would only be possible at the cost of an accelerating inflation rate. With such policies expectations would lag behind reality all the time (Sijben, 1979). It is the mechanism of adaptive expectations that gives politicians in the Nordhaus political business cycle model the opportunity to manipulate the Phillips curve economy. The inflationary consequences of expansionary policies become clear to economic subjects only after the elections (Keech, 1995).

in the long run, lower unemployment and higher inflation than is optimal.[6]

The results of Nordhaus's model led to suggestions to limit the possibility for democratic governments to execute economic policies. Negative consequences, or more precisely, suboptimal economic outcomes in public choice theory usually come down to higher inflation.[7] Barry (1991) discussed the political business cycle theory of Nordhaus and argued that permitting inflation is not an indication of the failure of democratic institutions. There is no evidence, according to Barry, that inflation conflicts with the preferences of voters. He concluded that the proposals for reforming democratic institutions stem from nineteenth-century economic liberals. For those economists, who have a prejudiced preference for the market and dislike state intervention, inflation is the excuse to propose balanced budgets, autonomous central banks, and so forth. Barry argued that monetarism, or market liberalism, conflicts with democracy. 'Anyone whose primary commitment is to the market must, therefore, look on the democratic state, with its inevitable tendency to regulate, make collective provision, and redistribute, with antipathy. The political problem facing that person is how to get democratic approval for tying the hands of elected governments in perpetuity' (Barry, 1991: 98; see also Przeworksi, 1990). In other words, according to Barry and Przeworski the methodological assumptions of public choice theory are based on ideology. Consequently, the recommendations follow from ideological biased theories. One of the alternatives Nordhaus suggested was to take away from the politicians the instruments of fiscal policy and

---

[6] Frey and Ramser (1976) questioned this result. In their view it depends on the assumption of myopic short-run policy of vote-maximization. Frey and Ramser showed that the result of Nordhaus cannot be maintained if it is assumed that governments want to maximize the length of time in power instead of vote-maximization. '*A purely myopic policy is not a general characteristic of governments in democracies*' (Frey and Ramser, 1976: 555, italics in original).

[7] Buchanan is probably the most important representative of normative public choice theorists. Based on methodological individualism - public choice theory is 'an individualistic theory of politics' (Buchanan, 1984: 12) - he came to the conclusion that democratic economic policy is inefficient. He argued for constitutional rules for government spending in order to prevent politicians from causing inefficient government deficits and to avoid the inflationary consequences of such policies (Buchanan and Wagner, 1978; Brennan and Buchanan, 1985).

to give them to a service of civil servants (similar to an independent central bank that is responsible for monetary policy).[8]

Since Nordhaus's article a substantial amount of work has been done to develop further models based on the principle of the political business cycle, and to find empirical evidence for such a pattern. Early examples are MacRae (1977) and Tufte (1978). MacRae developed a model, resembling Nordhaus's model, to demonstrate theoretically the potential in democratic societies for a stable political business cycle if voters are myopic. However, he also paid attention to strategic voting as a means of eliminating such a cycle. In MacRae's view rational voters, voting strategically, cannot be fooled by opportunistic election policies of an incumbent politician.

The political business cycle according to Nordhaus and MacRae takes the form of oscillations in inflation and unemployment. In contrast to this, Tufte focused mainly on fluctuations in real disposable income. 'Real disposable income, unlike other major aspects of aggregate economic performance (such as unemployment, inflation, or real growth), can be immediately and directly influenced by short-run government action through taxes and transfers with little uncertainty about the time lag between activation of the policy instruments and the resulting change in real disposable income' (Tufte, 1978: 10). In addition he made the often quoted statement: '... a sure way to increase the real disposable income of voters is to mail them larger checks' (Tufte, 1978: 38). Accordingly, Tufte focused in his research more on policy instruments than on economic outcomes. By doing so he implicitly recognized that it may be difficult for governments to influence economic outcomes, but that they will certainly try to manipulate the instruments at their disposal.

The search for empirical evidence The empirical evidence for the traditional political business cycle is inconclusive.[9] Nordhaus found

---

[8] Similar suggestions were made by Lindbeck (1976). In addition to 'depoliticization' (Lindbeck 1976: 18) both authors suggested possibilities for reform like broadening the base of participation in policy-making or improving the availability of information to voters (see for the complete list Nordhaus, 1975: 188 and Lindbeck, 1976: 18).

[9] This section describes the search for empirical evidence for the political business cycle theory. It does not present the actual results of this

evidence for such a pattern for three countries out of nine: Germany, the United States and New Zealand. There were some indications for France and Sweden, whereas the data for Australia, Canada, Japan and the United Kingdom did not indicate a pattern in accordance with political business cycles. McCallum (1978) tested the Nordhaus-model against the rational expectations theory of Sargent and Wallace (1975). According to the rational expectations hypothesis it is impossible for governments to exploit the Phillips curve. Using six different election variables - variables that are constructed to capture electoral politics - McCallum could not find evidence for a political business cycle in the United States (1948-1974). In contrast, the rational expectations hypothesis was not contradicted by the data.

Instead of concentrating on inflation and unemployment, Tufte (1978) considered incomes policies and a set of instruments that influence real disposable income. He found evidence for an electoral economic cycle in 19 of the 27 countries he examined. In these countries acceleration in real income growth occurred more often in election years than in years without an election.[10]

Despite the work of Tufte many authors are for many reasons sceptical about the existence of political business cycles: (i) because of the high costs involved politicians are not able to have the impact on the economy they would need to influence voters (Golden and Poterba, 1980); (ii) other economic factors are more important for short-run economic policies than opportunistic politicians, for example unexpected shocks, such as the oil crises of 1973 and 1979 (Whitely, 1986). Whiteley investigated the popularity and reaction of governments with respect to inflation and unemployment in the United States, the United Kingdom and the Federal Republic of Germany. He concluded that the long-run relation between politics and the economy is more important than the short-run interaction; (iii) other political factors are ignored by the political business cycle theory, for example ideology (Hibbs, 1987b; Frey, 1978a; see

---

empirical research. The reason is that the evidence is too inconclusive, that the variation in countries and time periods is too large, that too many different political and economic variables are used to warrant a useful comparison of the many empirical results.

[10] The Netherlands was one of the countries where he could not find an electoral economic cycle. For further evidence, see Tufte (1978).

section 1.3); (iv) voters and economic subjects are rational, and cannot be fooled by opportunistic politicians (McCallum, 1978; and see the section on the political business cycle with rational expectations); (v) as Alt and Chrystal (1983: 123) stated: 'Pre-election stimulation of the economy could be a strategy which may or may not be adopted, but no theory says why the strategy sometimes is and sometimes is not adopted'; and (vi) there is also no theory that explains why political business cycles could exist in one country, but not in another.

If there is evidence for political business cycles, it comes from research on large, more or less two-party democracies, notably the United States and sometimes the United Kingdom. But even in these countries it is not conclusive. Alt (1980) claimed that there is considerable lack of evidence for a regular political business cycle in Britain.[11] All in all, this discussion points to an extensive lack of evidence for a business cycle that is caused by the timing of elections.

Revival of the Nordhaus political business cycle? Due to the lack of evidence and due to the rational expectations revolution, research on political business cycle theory had decreased since the beginning of the 1980s. At the end of the 1980s, however, a new flow of publications on the Nordhaus-cycle began to emerge (in addition to the research on political economic models that incorporate rational expectations; see next section). Haynes and Stone (1989), reacting to the empirical research that had been done since the 1970s, maintained that political business cycles are significant, even strongly significant, for the United States (1951-1986). They used an integrated test, taking into account the difference between economic outcomes (gross domestic product (GDP), unemployment and inflation) and economic policies (money growth and the government budget). They argued that previous empirical research imposed arbitrary restrictions on electoral patterns by using arbitrary variables to capture electoral politics. For their empirical examination Haynes and Stone used election variables describing the total electoral

---

[11] There have been many investigations in other countries, for example in the Scandinavian countries. Madsen (1980) found strong indications for a political business cycle in unemployment and public expenditures in Norway, but found no evidence for Sweden. He explained this difference by referring to the tight labour market in Sweden.

period. These variables took into account the entire electoral period, that is, each quarter of an electoral period of four years.

However, further evidence provided by Haynes and Stone (1990) demonstrated an important difference between Republican and Democratic governments, for only for Republican governments significant electoral cycles were found. Democratic governments, with a majority in Congress, instead of fine tuning policy in order to win elections, are more able to pursue partisan goals, whereas, according to Haynes and Stone, the minority party, the Republican one, is less able to pursue partisan goals and, therefore, concentrates on policies that enhance its chance of re-election. Haynes and Stone thus established that political conditions affect the need or the ability for distinct governments to manufacture a political business cycle.

Haynes and Stone explicitly investigated monetary policy. There are more economists cited in the political business cycle literature who particularly investigated political motivated monetary policy. It is important to consider monetary policy for two reasons. Firstly, the manipulation of the growth of the money stock is important also in the case that fiscal policy is used to generate a political business cycle. Secondly, there is the question whether the central bank really operates independently or that monetary policy is influenced by government pressure. Grier (1987) examined a 'political monetary cycle' in the United States by testing it for an election cycle in money growth. He used six different variables to describe the electoral period of four years (16 quarters). Taking into account various economic parameters, different policy regimes and chairmen of the Federal Reserve System (Fed), he found a significant political effect on money growth in all the tests he performed.[12] In the year following an election there is a deceleration in money growth, whereas in the next three years there is an acceleration. Grier concluded that these results question the generally accepted belief in the independence of the Fed.[13]

Beck (1987, 1988) does not doubt that monetary policy is politically motivated. He noted that the aim to make central banks

---

[12] Testing for different policy regimes (Democratic or Republican presidents) and for different Fed chairmen was done by testing the political variables for subsamples of the total sample (1961-1982).

[13] For further discussion and more evidence, see Grier (1989).

independent from democratic politics is itself a political act. The question is how monetary policy is affected by politics. It may be that the president (in the United States) does not have the power to force a politically motivated monetary policy on the Fed, but does the Fed counteract non-monetary presidential manipulation? According to Beck (1987) the Fed does not counterbalance cycles in the quantity of money that are not caused by the Fed.

Haynes and Stone questioned the empirical design of the analysis of the political factor. However, it is also possible to criticize the theoretical modelling of the assumed behaviour of politicians. Whereas the behaviour of economic subjects and voters, and in general the economic theory of the original political business cycle, has been seriously questioned, the behaviour of politicians in these kinds of models has remained the same since the 1970s; for every election politicians behave opportunistic, resulting in predictable political business cycles (Schultz, 1995). In Schultz's opinion this political behaviour entails serious costs. It could lead to a poorer future macroeconomic performance and it damages the reputation of a politician or political party. Therefore, rational incumbent politicians will only display such a behaviour when there is a political need to do so. In the empirical studies of Schultz of British transfer payments (1961-1992) political need is measured by opinion poll data just before the elections. In this way Schultz follows the research by Frey and Schneider (1978a and b; see section 1.3), who were the first to take account of opinion polls in political economic models. For transfer payments in Great Britain Schultz did not find evidence to substantiate the existence of the original political business cycle. In contrast, the model which takes account of the electoral situation, in terms of opinion poll data, performed better empirically: the timing of elections significantly influences transfer payments when incumbent politicians feel electorally endangered.

In 1989 Nordhaus himself wrote a paper reviewing the research that had been done on political business cycles since he had started the discussion about them in 1975. He defended the theoretical underpinnings of his original theory.[14] He also offered empirical evidence and examples to support his view. For the United States there is evidence for an influence of elections on unemployment. Elections have had their

---

[14] He defended the original political business cycle especially against the partisan cycle theory and against the rational expectations critique.

influence on past fiscal policies (especially the 1972 Nixon elections). Monetary policies, in contrast, seem not to be controlled by electoral politics (the only exception being the elections of 1972). However, Nordhaus acknowledged that elections are not the only political variable that might have an effect on the economy or on economic policy. Partisan goals can also have an impact, although a large effect for the ideological variable was not found in his empirical research (and it was less significant than the election or opportunistic variable). Still, Nordhaus concluded that is possible to have a variety of political cycles. There could even exist a self-correcting mechanism. For example, after the elections of 1972 measures were taken to make it more difficult for the government to use fiscal policies or monetary policies by the Fed (under government pressure), for electoral reasons. Consequently, the electoral political business cycle may have become more difficult to establish for political parties. In Nordhaus's view, however, this does not imply that the political business cycle is dead. 'The primordial political forces that originally produced political cycles are as vigorous as ever. Hence, like any evolving creature, the political business cycle is likely to emerge in the future in unexpected shapes and with unanticipated dynamics' (Nordhaus, 1989: 49). In other words, the opportunistic mechanism exists, but its shape may transform.

The Political Business Cycle with Rational Expectations

Following Alesina a distinction can be made between two periods of research on political economic cycles. This holds for political business cycles as well as for partisan cycles (see Alesina, 1988, 1995; Alesina, Cohen and Roubini, 1993).[15] An important criticism of the political economic cycles literature of the 1970s came from the adherents of the rational expectations theory. The early theories of political business cycles were based on an exploitable Phillips curve and the assumption of myopic voters, which are assumptions that were severely attacked by rational expectations economists. New classicals, such as Lucas (1973) and

---

[15] Alesina has the habit of writing excellent overviews of the literature. See, for example, Alesina (1988, 1989, 1995), Alesina and Roubini (1992), Alesina, Cohen and Roubini (1993) and Alesina and Rosenthal (1995). An equally excellent survey of the modern literature on economics and politics is given by Keech (1995).

Sargent and Wallace (1975), argued that even in the short-term there is no Phillips curve trade-off between inflation and employment. With perfect markets and rational economic agents only unexpected policy shocks may have temporary real effects, at the cost of higher inflation. Following on the rational expectations augmented Phillips curve theory, Kydland and Prescott, who were among the first to use game theory in the field of macroeconomic policy research, showed that policy rules for economic policy are better than discretionary policies. According to these authors rational expectations and optimal stabilization policy are incompatible because of time inconsistency of policies. They concluded that 'active stabilization may very well be dangerous and it is best that it is not attempted' (Kydland and Prescott, 1977: 407).

Since the 1980s authors such as Barro and Gordon (1983, 1985), Cukierman and Meltzer (1986), Alesina (1987), Rogoff and Sibert (1988) and Rogoff (1990) have tried to incorporate rational expectations in their game theoretical political economic theories. In their view political business cycles may arise because of temporary information asymmetries. Voters are assumed to vote rationally, and are therefore not misled as they are in the Nordhaus-model. Yet, they do not have perfect information about for example the proficiency of the contesting political parties (Rogoff and Sibert, 1988; Rogoff, 1990). For this reason incumbent politicians will try, by choosing clearly discernible policies, to signal to voters that they are competent. Rogoff constructed a theory in which a political business cycle occurs in fiscal instruments. He named this cycle the political budget cycle. Taxes and transfers are policy instruments which politicians employ for their signalling game, although they know that there are no real economic effects to be expected from their policies.[16]

The search for empirical evidence Alesina and Roubini (1992) tested the political business cycle theory against partisan theories for 18 OECD democracies (1960-1987). There was no evidence for an electoral cycle in

---

[16] Because of learning effects of rational voters the patterns are not as systematic as the original political business cycles suggest (Alesina and Rosenthal, 1995). For an overview of the literature on this topic, and an extension of the theory, see Persson and Tabellini (1990). For a more sophisticated survey of modern political business cycle models, see Gärtner (1994).

the growth of gross domestic product (GDP) and unemployment. Alesina, Cohen and Roubini (1992, 1993) explicitly re-examined the influence of elections on macroeconomic policy (for the same sample and sample period). Their conclusions were that there is 'little evidence of pre-electoral effects on economic outcomes' (GDP growth and unemployment), that there is 'some evidence of "political monetary cycles"', that there are 'indications of "political budget cycles"' and that 'inflation exhibits a post-electoral jump' (Alesina, Cohen and Roubini, 1992: 1). The data showed mixed, but interesting results for separate countries. An electoral cycle pattern for GDP growth was found for the United Kingdom, Germany, New Zealand and Japan. Germany and New Zealand are also two countries that fitted the theory in Nordhaus (1975). For most of the countries an effect was found on inflation, except for the Netherlands. According to the authors a jump in inflation after the elections could be explained by the use of policy instruments before the elections. They found evidence for an electoral cycle in monetary (money growth) as well as fiscal policy (debt ratio). Germany was again one of the countries where a significant monetary cycle was found, which is very remarkable because the Bundesbank is assumed to be one of the most autonomous central banks in the world (Alesina, Cohen and Roubini, 1992).

Alesina, Cohen and Roubini (1993) provided further evidence particularly on manipulation of policy instruments (taxation and spending). The results are comparable with their earlier test report. Important is their reiteration of a point already made by Lindbeck (1976) that 'pre-electoral opportunistic behavior for left wing governments may be different than that of right wing governments. ... left wing governments, who at the beginning of their administration pursued expansionary monetary policies to lower unemployment, may be reducing money growth at the end of their terms, to bring down the inflation caused by their initial expansionary policies. Conversely, right wing governments, who undertook contractionary monetary policy to lower inflation, may be expanding at the end of their terms of office' (Alesina, Cohen and Roubini, 1993: 14).

As noted in the introduction to this chapter, the literature on political business cycles is vast. Moreover, the discussion about their empirical relevance and theoretical construction is still in progress. It is clear from this short overview of existing empirical investigations that no obvious conclusions can be drawn with respect to the existence of political business cycles. The argument that governments would want to try to manipulate economic outcomes or economic policy instruments to enhance electoral chances, remains persuasive, but the pattern may not be as systematic as implied by political business cycle models. Or, as Nordhaus stated, it may be changing over time. In chapter three it is examined whether the theory of political business cycles has any empirical relevance for the Dutch economy.

1.3 The Partisan Theory

Political factors are important for explaining economic outcomes. Political business cycles may occur because of pre-election stimulation of the economy. Economic policy is enforced by electorally motivated politicians. However, to quote Locksley, 'party competition is non-existent. Oppositions do not win elections; only incumbents lose them when they get their timing wrong' (Locksley, 1980: 184). Apart from political business cycles, which may occur with all political parties, a partisan cycle may exist. This cycle reflects that different political parties have different economic objectives. Consequently, a change in government control determines a change in economic policy and economic outcomes. Politicians are not (only) electorally motivated, they are (also) motivated by ideology.

Hibbs's Partisan Cycle

Hibbs was one of the first to examine partisan models (Hibbs, 1977a). He concluded that 'the macroeconomic policies pursued by left and right-wing governments are broadly in accordance with the objective economic interests and subjective preferences of their class-defined core political constituencies' (Hibbs, 1977a: 1467). To come to this conclusion he made the following assumptions: (i) 'price stability and full employment are incompatible goals' (p. 1468); (ii) 'low and middle income and occupational status groups are more averse to unemployment than inflation, whereas, upper income and occupational status groups are more concerned about inflation than unemployment' (p. 1470). Hibbs based this difference in 'subjective preferences' on public opinion data from Great Britain and the United States; (iii) referring to empirical evidence for a profit squeeze type of argument, he stated that 'the evidence does demonstrate that the economic position of wage and salary earners as a group improves substantially, both in relative and absolute terms, during periods of relatively low unemployment and high inflation' (p. 1469). This means that there are also differences in objective economic goals; and (iv) political parties have different constituencies: 'the mass constituencies of political parties in most advanced industrial societies are distinguished to a significant extent by class, income, and related socioeconomic characteristics' (p. 1471). Allowing for an adaptation process, Hibbs's partisan cycle implies that governments can choose their preferred point on the Phillips curve. Left-wing governments will choose a situation with lower unemployment and higher inflation than right-wing governments. Alternating partisan governments will, therefore, cause a partisan cycle in macroeconomic performance. As Keech (1995) noted, it was the Phillips curve in Keynesian macroeconomics of the 1960s which provided the point of departure for analysing political economic interaction.

Since Hibbs's article many doubts have been raised about its empirical validity and many theoretical refinements have been introduced into the model. Political and social scientists using the comparative method (for example, Cameron, 1978; Castles, 1982a), and, again, also economists interested in rational expectations, became interested in the partisan composition of governments (for example, Alesina, 1987). The comparative research and the partisan theory with rational expectations are reviewed later on, but first some contributions are considered here which are more directly related to Hibbs's theory.

Empirical evidence and theoretical discussion Using cross national data from twelve countries Hibbs found some evidence of the predicted correlation between years of Socialist-Labour governments and inflation on the one hand and between Socialist-Labour governments and unemployment on the other. More convincing, however, is the evidence from time-series analysis of British and American data. For the unemployment model of Great Britain he found an inter-party difference in unemployment levels of 0.62 percent.[17] For the United States he found

---

[17] This was measured nett of trends, seasonal dependencies and stochastic fluctuations in the time series and nett of the effect of the introduction of a new unemployment compensation law in 1966 (see Hibbs, 1977a: 1481).

a difference of 2.36 percent.[18] That the equilibrium unemployment levels of Conservatives and Labour vary less than the unemployment levels of Republicans and Democrats is explained by the greater openness of the British economy and the constraints this imposes on macroeconomic policy.

Beck (1982) challenged Hibbs's conclusions for the United States, arguing, and empirically demonstrating, that inter-administration differences - differences between the successive governments regardless of their political descent - are more important for explaining unemployment than party goals. Beck was especially interested in the administrations that deviate from the behaviour predicted by the partisan theory of Hibbs: the Democratic Kennedy and Carter administrations and the Republican Nixon administration. However, Beck still found some room for a partisan effect, although it is limited to about half of the effect Hibbs found. Beck noted that the view of politics in Hibbs's paper 'is that the two major parties represent the major factions in society, with the division falling roughly along class lines and being relatively stable over time'. And further: 'the major fights occur at election time' (Beck, 1982: 92). In contrast, Beck adopted a view on politics that is based on pressure groups which struggle for control over the political parties. In this view 'parties represent differing combinations of groups at differing times' and 'politics consists of a series of impermanent coalitions between the various sectors of society, with elections offering a choice between temporary alliances. Party label is a guide to what these alliances look like ... but it is only a very imperfect guide' (Beck, 1982: 93).

An interesting paper that ought to be mentioned here is by Alt (1985). Like Beck, Alt tried to refine the partisan theory set out by Hibbs. Perhaps it could be said that he amended Hibbs's partisan model on two main points. Firstly, he explicitly took account of the fact that partisan economic policies have to be pursued within the context of a world economy. The openness of an economy and the level of economic activity on world markets constrain the freedom to pursue internal policies. Secondly, he tried to incorporate strategic elements into the political sector of the theory. He distinguished between situations where partisan effects on unemployment will be sustained, transitory or absent.

---

[18] In the unemployment model of the United States Hibbs introduced a war variable to take account of the economic effects of the American intervention in Korea and Vietnam.

Next to being dependent on economic constraints this depends on whether or not certain effects were promised before the elections, whether or not there is a dominant party or party-coalition and whether or not a government has a majority in parliament. The first argument is an explicitly politically strategic one, whereas the following two arguments are more of an institutional character. The institutional context is of course important for political strategy; consider for example the difference in party strategics in a two-party system or a coalition democracy. Both sorts of arguments are often neglected in models of political economic interaction. The institutional context will be returned to in section 1.4. First a comment on political strategy.

Alt incorporated (re-)election goals in his partisan model. To pursue partisan policies a party has to have control of government. Electoral considerations can therefore constrain partisan politics. The first authors who actually integrated both partisan goals and election goals in one model were Frey and Schneider (1978a and b).[19] They formulated a popularity function that determines whether or not there is electoral room for partisan policies. In their models for the United States and the United Kingdom there are two possibilities. There is either a situation of excess popularity, which means that the chance of being re-elected is high enough for a president to pursue ideological goals, or there is a situation of a popularity deficit. In that case the president or, in the case of the United Kingdom, the government, will have to undertake expansionary measures to increase the chances for re-election. Frey and Schneider found some evidence in support of their model. However, they recognized that the model is simple and 'at best a first step towards the formulation of a realistic approach to politico-economic interdependence' (Frey and Schneider, 1978a: 181).[20] Nevertheless, Frey and Schneider showed that it is possible to combine the arguments of the partisan models and the election models. The argument used in the Nordhaus-model as well as the argument used in the Hibbs-model is appealing. A combination of both

---

[19] See also Frey (1978a and b).

[20] Some more evidence is presented in Frey and Schneider (1980). Popularity functions were considered for both the United States and the Federal Republic of Germany. An example of further work on the topic is Borooah and Van der Ploeg (1983).

seems to be a logical strategy for building political economic interaction models.[21]

In general the empirical evidence for partisan cycles is more convincing than it is for political business cycles. As can be concluded from Beck's discussion of Hibbs's theory it is more a matter of intensity than a question whether politics matters or not.[22] The 1977 paper by Hibbs was mainly aimed at distinct partisan unemployment goals. More evidence was provided in later work (Hibbs, 1987a and 1987b).[23] The research was extended to other macroeconomic goals as well as to macroeconomic policies. It is not surprising that he found interparty differences in monetary and fiscal policies, for he already estimated differences in macroeconomic outcomes: for the United States (1953-1983) an interparty variation in unemployment of about two percentage points and a variation in real output of about six percent. Hibbs (1977a) argued that unemployment has negative distributional consequences for lower income groups. Policies aimed to reduce unemployment, with higher inflation, therefore have an equalizing effect on the income

---

[21] According to Havrilesky it may even be the case that redistributive partisan policies, which may alienate some groups of voters, may be accompanied by electorally motivated monetary policies to enhance the electoral chances of incumbents (Havrilesky, 1987 and 1988).

[22] Perhaps the strongest doubts about whether or not parties make a difference were raised by Rose (1980) for the case of Great Britain. Rose explained the difficulty of making a difference by factors as the intra-party policy discussions on many important issues (consensus has to be found among various points of view within a party), the dependency on the international economy, and electoral motives. He maintained that 'British parties tend to behave in Consensus terms because they owe their position to popular election, and the British electorate tends towards agreement rather than disagreement on major issues' (Rose, 1980: 143). Hibbs (1982) in an analysis of British political economics came to an opposite conclusion: 'the argument that there has been a persistent decline of class-based political alignments in Britain is erroneous' (Hibbs, 1982: 259). Brenner and Brenner-Golomb (1996) are also convinced that ideology does not matter in formulating economic policies. All politicians or political parties pursue economic policies to win elections, irrespective of proclaimed ideology.

[23] Both are collections of essays summarizing for about a decade Hibbs's work on political economic interaction.

distribution. However, Hibbs (1987b) stated that beside the indirect effect of macroeconomic performance there are also direct effects on income distribution through the partisan policies of taxes and transfers (see also Tufte, 1978). For the United States he found an interparty difference in the equalizing effect of (Democratic) social security programs. He concluded: 'the course of redistributive policies and outcomes during the post war period, then, is one of Democratic initiatives that successfully (though modestly) moved toward equality, followed by periods of Republican inaction, followed by new Democratic efforts to improve the relative position of low-income groups, and so on' (Hibbs, 1987b: 239).

Partisan Cycles with Rational Expectations

As previously noted, the literature on partisan cycles may be divided into the literature from the 1970s and early 1980s and the literature from later dates. Because of the rational expectations critique on the early political economic models, various authors tried to incorporate rational expectations in their models. Alesina (1987) developed a game theoretical partisan model with rational voters and rational wage-setters. Using a Lucas-supply function he demonstrated that differences in inflation and unemployment can still occur because of uncertain election outcomes.

As Alesina and Rosenthal (1995) noted, rational partisan cycles take an eclectic point of view regarding macroeconomic theory. In these models the rational expectations hypothesis of the new classicals is combined with game-theoretic time inconsistency and neo-Keynesian wage-price rigidities. The two political parties are assumed to have different time-consistent policy rules. That is, the parties are assumed to follow different policies despite the fact that economic policy has no real effects. This is caused by the assumption that a low inflation objective of the left-wing party is not credible. If a low inflation objective of a left-wing party would be considered to be credible, this party would have an incentive and an opportunity to cause a policy shock, resulting in real, but transitory, economic effects. Next to the assumption about the policy rules, the rational expectations partisan theory assumes that nominal wage-contracts are signed before the election (wage-price rigidity). These assumptions and the uncertainty about the outcome of the general election provide the necessary policy shock in a rational world explaining the pattern of rational partisan cycles. In non-election years wage-setters set the wage at the rational expected inflation rate and are not surprised.

It is rather strange, however, that in this rational world rational wage-setters make wage contracts before the elections. If they wait with signing contracts until after the elections they will not encounter the electoral surprise that causes the partisan effects in this model (see also Hibbs, 1992 and Rogoff, 1988). The search for a way to incorporate rational expectations in political economic models seems obsessive. Nevertheless, the empirical implications are interesting. Despite rational expectations, Alesina's theory predicts inter-party differences in inflation and unemployment.[24] Empirically his theory means that interparty differences in unemployment typically occur in the first year after elections.

The search for empirical evidence Alesina, with various collaborators, thoroughly tested the variants of political economic interaction with rational expectations. Alesina and Sachs (1988) examined such a model for monetary policy in the United States. They found that real effects of monetary policy only occur immediately after elections. With rational expectations about the different policies the two political parties will employ after an electoral victory, the uncertainty of election results and, thus, the uncertainty about which policies will be employed provides the possibility of a policy shock that is needed in these kinds of models to obtain real effects. As predicted by the theory, Alesina and Sachs found an interparty difference in the growth of GDP in the two years following an election. Money growth is different for the whole administration period (time consistent). These results were found for the United States by regression analysis with binary variables for Democratic and Republican governments and a variable referring to the second half of a republican government to capture the distinction between the first and the second half of an administration (1949-1984). The results were not strongly significant.[25]

---

[24] For another prominent theoretical partisan model incorporating rational expectations, see Chappell and Keech (1986a and b).

[25] Neither the Kennedy nor the Nixon administration fit the theory. Alesina and Sachs ascribed this to an expansionary policy combined with a tight money policy during the Kennedy administration and to a policy regime during the Nixon administration that may better be explained by a political business cycle.

Alesina (1988) provided further evidence on the partisan model of monetary policy for the United States. In the model specifications of money growth he also took account of other economic variables, namely the rate of unemployment, the difference with a computed natural rate of unemployment, real output growth and the difference with a computed potential output. The results were significant and in accordance with the theory. The testing of autoregressive specifications of unemployment and output indicated an empirical superiority of the Alesina model as compared to the partisan model of Hibbs and the political business cycle of Nordhaus. Alesina and Roubini (1992) found similar results with panel regressions for 18 OECD economies.

In an overview of the research on partisan theory, Hibbs (1992) discussed the empirical results of Alesina and collaborators. Hibbs especially criticized the fact that the central hypothesis of the rational partisan theory - the uncertainty about the results of elections - was not tested. According to Hibbs it is often the case that the uncertainty about election results is limited, which would mean, according to the rational expectations hypothesis, that there can be no partisan differences in macroeconomic performance at all.

To conclude, it seems logical that ideological preferences of partisan governments influence economic policy and affect the economy. The evidence reported in the literature seems more convincing than that of the political business cycle models. Nevertheless, the literature does report mixed results of empirical research of partisan models. Perhaps these kinds of models are too mechanistic to explain the influence of ideology on economic policy. For example, the models do not take account of the institutional context in which the government decides on economic policies. Therefore, in the next section an entirely different branch of research on political economic interaction is discussed. In the theories of this research attention is given to other institutionalized actors, such as the labour movement.

1.4 Institutional Interaction

Critics of the mainstream variant of modern political economy claim that this approach has both theoretical and empirical shortcomings. Too much attention is given to mathematical theory and too little to empirical research in order to test the practical relevance of these theories. A major part of public choice theory, the mainstream variant of modern political economy, is indeed mainly theoretical and extremely abstract (see, for example, the textbook by Mueller, 1989), although many of the models of political economic interaction discussed in the earlier sections were tested empirically. Especially the theory of the political business cycle is an example of public choice theory.

In the introduction reference was already made to the distinction between two approaches to modern political economy: the economics of politics approach, referring especially to public choice theory, and the politics of economics approach (Hemerijck, 1992, 1994b). The economics of politics uses neo-classical economic theory to analyse politics or political economic mechanisms. The main characteristic of the political business cycle theory, part of the economics of politics, is its reductionist point of view. Based on the calculations of rational individuals this theory intends to demonstrate the (in-)efficiency of democratic institutions. It is a highly mechanistic theory of one possible aspect of politically motivated economic policies. Other social or political realities play no role in this theory. In economic theory the kinds of assumptions used by political business cycle theory are encapsulated by the term methodological individualism.

In the partisan models the situation is somewhat more complex. In these models political interaction is not reduced to individual preferences. It is the preferences of classes or distinct income groups that determine economic policy of different partisan governments. Politicians have no preferences of their own. They just act on the interests of the constituency and voters of their political party. In other words, their preferences are the same as the parties' preferences, they are 'identical' (Alesina and Rosenthal, 1995: 19). However, the macroeconomic aspects of the rational partisan theory are characterized by reductionism. The rational expectations hypothesis constitutes the micro foundation of macroeconomic theory. In other words, the macroeconomic outcomes are determined by rational economic subjects interacting on perfect markets; the economic behaviour of individuals determines the success of politically motivated economic policies. Thus, the partisan theory is difficult to classify. Hibbs's theory may be classified as part of the politics of economics approach, whereas it may be more suitable to classify the models of Alesina as part of the economics of politics approach.

Theories of the politics of economics are discussed in the present section. These theories study collective entities and stress the importance of power considerations. It uses a comparative methodology. In contrast to the economics of politics, which focuses on political mechanisms, the politics of economics analyses the differences in economic performance by looking at the institutional differences between countries. Hemerijck (1994b) explained that the politics of economics approach is above all empirically oriented. The research questions arise from real world problems. The most important theme of research is the economic crisis of the 1970s. Politics of economics authors observed a diverging macroeconomic performance of the OECD countries in the 1970s and early 1980s. The hypothesis emerged that this divergence may be explained by distinct institutional structures of countries, for example, distinct political institutions. The idea is that the institutional structure of a country determines how economic policy is formulated. Consequently, different institutional contexts lead to different economic policies and lead to diverging macroeconomic performances. By using the comparative method to investigate these kinds of hypotheses the politics of economics is empirically oriented, and pays less attention to theoretical economic arguments. Two themes have a prominent place in this approach: (i) the impact of parties on the economy; and (ii) corporatist structures and economic performance. Both themes are interrelated.

First some general remarks are made about comparative political economics. The debate about corporatism dominates this branch of research. It is explained how economic policy is decided upon in a corporatist institutional structure, and how this structure affects economic performance. Subsequently some theories are discussed focusing on the interaction between political actors such as political parties and the labour movement. The institutional structure in these theories is less important than in the corporatism theories. It is the strategic interaction between the political actors that explains economic performance. Economic policy of partisan governments depends on the interaction with the labour movement and the employers' organizations. In this sense these organizations determine the institutional context in which political parties in government have to decide on economic policy. Specific economic and political circumstances are of importance in these theories.

Comparative Political Economics

A substantial part of the politics of economics approach is made up of comparative political economics. Using the comparative method this branch of research is interested in the varying macroeconomic performance of democratic capitalist economies in relation to the institutional structure of these countries. Corporatist structures and the partisan compòsition of governments are the centre of attention in the research programme of comparative political economy.[26] For the purpose of this book the role of political parties is of special importance.

Corporatism, 'usually accompanied by some prefix such as "neo", "liberal", or "quasi"' (Cameron, 1984: 145),[27] became a major theme in political economic research in the 1970s. Although the precise concept or definition of corporatism is much discussed (see, for example, Schmitter, 1979; Panitch, 1980; Cameron, 1984) it can be maintained, following Lehmbruch (1984), that the following three elements are of importance: (i) the existence of centralized interest organizations which have, as Lehmbruch labelled it, representational monopoly; (ii) these interest organizations are linked with public administration; and (iii) there is a social partnership of labour and business. These three elements are central in the concept of corporatism. However, there is no consensus about the scope of the concept. Woldendorp (1995) suggested that the contributions to the corporatism debate may be classified into different categories. He distinguished between perceptions of corporatism as a system, as a structure or as a strategy.[28] In short, the system approach perceives

---

[26] The literature on corporatism is vast. Already in 1980 Panitch used the term 'growth industry' for the expansion of literature on this topic. In this section an attempt is made to survey the most important contributions. However, there is no guarantee that the survey is complete. For a recent survey of theories of institutions of economic policy-making, see Van Waarden (1997).

[27] 'Democratic' is another often used prefix to distinguish the modern version of the concept of corporatism from the one that was affiliated with fascism earlier this century.

[28] Beside this classification, Woldendorp categorizes the contributions to the debate with respect to the level of corporatist interaction into the macro or the meso level. In the present book only the macro level - the national level on which economic policy is decided upon by the government and interest groups - is

corporatism as an economic system next to socialism or capitalism; the structure approach understands corporatism as a structure of political, economic and social relations within a capitalist democracy; and, finally, the strategy approach sees corporatism as a way of confronting economic problems. The first two approaches stress the importance of the existence of the institutional elements determining whether a country is a corportist country or not. The strategy approach focuses more on strategic interaction between institutional actors to determine whether or not economic problems (economic crises) are confronted by way of corporatist cooperation. Strategic interaction is discussed later on. First some attention is paid to various contributions to the corporatism debate in general.

Authors such as Schmitter (1981) and Lehner (1987) analysed corporatism as a way of institutionalized governing (in policy networks) with interest groups interacting with the government (interest intermediation). Lehmbruch (1984) named such an institutional framework in which policy is tripartite formulated a framework of concertation. 'Concerted' policies are developed and implemented in an institutional setting where centralized interest organizations are linked with public administration and where there is a kind of social partnership between labour and business (Lehmbruch, 1984: 64). Lehmbruch and Lehner stressed the importance of the organization of interest organizations for corporatism, but do not attach too much importance to the partisan composition of governments. Corporatist networks in their view serve to build consensus among political parties. Moreover, according to Lehmbruch stable corporatist patterns of economic and social policy are 'not compatible with party conflict in these same areas' (Lehmbruch, 1984: 77). Corporatism, therefore, neutralizes party competition and, as Lehmbruch noted, 'served to smooth out the "political business cycle"' (Lehmbruch, 1984: 74).[29] At the same time governments are willing to follow corporatist politics in order to avoid major societal conflicts and

---

discussed. The meso or sectoral level is neglected.

[29] Moreover, it is the leaders of the political parties who cooperate with each other to build political consensus. Such a democracy, where the decisions are taken by the political elite, is called a consociational democracy (Lehmbruch, 1979).

conflicts between the government and the labour unions (Armingeon, 1987).

Corporatism in this sense implies an institutional system or structure determining the way in which economic policy is decided upon. It is not clear how a country becomes a corporatist country. A strong (and centralized) labour movement seems a prerequisite for corporatist national policy making. To explain the existence of such strong labour movements requires a historical analysis.[30] Apart from historical explanations, however, Cameron (1978) and especially Katzenstein (1983, 1985) provided interesting argumentation for the existence of corporatist policy making in various countries.

According to both authors it is the small open economies in Western Europe which are institutionally organized according to the corporatist model. Corporatism is seen as the political strategy for small open economies to confront the needs of international competition.[31] According to Katzenstein protectionism is not a viable strategy for small economies. To be successful in a large and ever changing world market the openness and vulnerability of such countries demands a flexible national policy of industrial adjustments. In different forms of corporatism (social or liberal democratic corporatism) countries cope with such policies, at the same time compensating the costs of adjustment policies. 'The political requirements of democratic corporatism account for the adoption of wide ranging policies of domestic compensation by the small European states' (Katzenstein, 1985: 133). Cameron noted: 'governments in small open economies have tended to provide a variety of income supplements in the form of social security schemes, health insurance, unemployment benefits, job training, employment subsidies to firms, and even investment capital' (Cameron, 1978: 1260). To conclude: 'the small European states have learned how to live with the costs of change' (Katzenstein, 1985: 134).

It is not often that political economists explain national politics in an international context. However, Katzenstein tended to neglect national party politics. Political parties do not really play a part in his theory. But

---

[30] For an explanation of historical institutionalism in comparative political economics, see Thelen and Steinmo (1992).

[31] Here strategy is not seen as the way in which short-term policy choices are made, but a long-term institutional development of policy structures.

he cannot explain the different strategies of different small European economies. According to Czada (1987) political parties and party politics may explain different policy choices among small economies: 'the impact of interest organizations on policies should not be isolated from party politics, in particular party-group linkages, governmental strategies and national bureaucratic styles' (Czada, 1987: 46). Czada especially referred to the different strategies followed by respectively Social Democratic and Christian Democratic parties.

In relation to corporatist institutional structures Marxist authors and authors especially interested in Social Democracy stress the importance of the strength of political parties in general and the political strength of labour in particular (see for example Korpi, 1983; Cameron, 1978, 1984; Schmidt, 1982). According to these authors it is the combination of corporatist policy making together with left control of the government that may have positive consequences for the economy. Some authors, however, question the beneficial consequences of corporatism. 'Are the interests of labour in fact represented when leftist parties govern and/or when labour participates in corporatist arrangements? Or are leftist governments and corporatist arrangements simply forms by which labour is coopted, compromised, controlled, and subordinated?' (Cameron, 1984: 145). Some Marxist authors tend to answer this second question affirmatively. In discussing the various definitions of corporatism Cameron concluded: 'in short, corporatism can be seen as a system of institutionalized wage restraint in which labour, acting "responsibly", voluntarily participates and legitimizes the transfer of income from labour to capital' (Cameron, 1984: 146). Miliband used this same quotation to discuss the second question of Cameron. Granting that corporatism in Social Democratic Sweden worked well as a political strategy, he maintained that in other countries, of course using Britain as an example, 'corporatist policies have meant above all else wage restraint and other sacrifices for the working class.' And further: 'for in societies which are class-divided and class-competitive, and in which labour movements are not nearly so well entrenched as in Sweden, the restraint of trade union power is much more likely to serve the interests of employers and of the dominant class in general than "the general economic interest"' (Miliband, 1991: 128).

Marxists fear the sacrifices made by labour unions' participation in corporatist agreements. However, as Castles, among others, pointed out, there are also gains for the labour unions: economic stability, full employment, economic growth, high social wage (Castles, 1987). Most authors do therefore not immediately assign such a normative judgment to corporatist interaction between the government, organized labour and employers. It is precisely assumed that there is 'a strong interdependence between the interests of conflicting social groups in a capitalist economy' (Lehmbruch, 1979: 55).

Political economists usually distinguish between progressive left-wing control of the government and conservative right-wing control. There are only a few authors to recognize the special role for Catholic or confessional political parties. In discussing corporatist structures Wilensky (1984) found that there are no differences between left-wing parties and Catholic parties with respect to the amount of welfare spending. As a matter of fact, corporatism seems to fit very well with Catholic ideology: harmonizing conflicting interests of rival groups with an active role of the state (Wilensky, 1984).[32] A comprehensive theory about different forms of welfare states was put forward by Esping-Andersen (1990). Using his concept of 'decomodification',[33] which is a measure for the degree in which citizens for their living standards are dependent on market forces, he made a distinction between 'three worlds of welfare capitalism': a Liberal, a Conservative (including countries with a strong Catholic dominance) and a Social Democratic welfare state. These three kinds of, more or less corporatist, welfare states have their particular welfare state arrangements with as distinguishing criterium the different roles of the state and the market in welfare provisions. With regard to corporatism he noted: 'for the Catholic Church, corporatism was a natural response to its preoccupation with preserving the traditional family, its search for viable alternatives to both socialism and capitalism, and its belief in the possibility of organizing harmonious relations between the social classes. Corporatism inserted itself easily into Catholicism's "subsidiarity" principle, the idea that higher and larger levels of social collectivity should only intervene when the family's capacity for mutual protection was rendered impossible' (Esping-Andersen, 1990: 61).

---

[32] This does not mean that all their policies are the same. Wilensky pointed out that there is, for example, a difference in preferences with regard to the tax structure. Leftist parties favour progressive, visible taxes, whereas Catholic parties try to avoid such taxes and prefer indirect taxing.

[33] See also Esping-Andersen and Korpi (1984).

As described by Lehmbruch (1984) and Armingeon (1987), corporatism is a way of political pacification, mainly in countries with large and centralized labour movements. Apart from the organization of the labour movement the political colour is of importance. There seems to be a difference between various types of corporatism dependent of the political colour of governments. The differences between these various types of corporatism are important for comparative research. It may explain varying economic policies better than the simple distinction between corporatist or non-corporatist countries. However, in this book not too much attention is given to the influence of Catholicism or Christian Democracy on economic policies. In the following chapters the political influences on the Dutch economy are examined. In this examination the focus is on the difference between centre-left and centre-right governments. Although Christian Democracy is important in the Netherlands (see Van Kersbergen, 1995; Woldendorp, 1993), this disregard is permitted because the research is not aimed at a comparison of various corporatist countries, but is an examination of political influences on the Dutch economy only.

Empirical research Despite theoretical differences, most authors hypothesized a positive relationship between economic performance (varying from economic growth and employment to strike level and income distribution) and corporatist structures. Some authors explicitly examined the significance of the partisan composition of governments in relation to corporatist structures. Here are some examples.

To measure comparatively the impact of corporatism on economic performance it is necessary to create a rank order of countries with varying degrees of corporatism. There are a number of authors who developed such a rank order. In table 1.1, which is based on two tables from Hemerijck (1992), these rankings are brought together.[34] The rankings are composed on the basis of, among other things, the degree of unionization, the centralization of labour unions, the degree of collective bargaining, institutionalized bi- and tripartite linkages (see for further attributes, Hemerijck, 1992). It is clear that there exists some variation in

---

[34] The rankings can be found in Wilensky (1976), Schmitter (1981), Cameron (1984), Bruno and Sachs (1985), Calmfors and Driffill (1988), Lehmbruch (1984) and Schmidt (1982).

these ranking orders. For example, the ranking of the Netherlands varies from strong to medium corporatism.

Table 1.1   **Rankings of corporatism**

Country	Wilensky	Schmitter	Cameron	Bruno Sachs	Calmfors Driffill	Lehmbruch	Schmidt
Austria	7	1	1	1	1	strong	strong
Germany	10	8	7	2	6	medium	medium
Netherlands	2	6	8	3	7	strong	medium
Norway	3	2	3	4	2	strong	strong
Sweden	4	4	2	5	3	strong	strong
Switzerland	11	9	9	6	14	medium	strong
Denmark	9	4	5	8	4	medium	medium
Finland	6	4	5	8	5	medium	medium
Belgium	1	7	6	9	8	-	-
Japan	-	-	14	10	13	weak	-
UK	12	14	10	11	11	weak	weak
Ireland	14	11	-	-	-	medium	weak
Canada	13	11	12	15	16	weak	weak
Australia	-	-	11	14	9	weak	-
New Zealand	-	-	-	-	-	weak	-
USA	15	11	13	16	15	weak	weak
Italy	8	15	15	13	12	weak	weak
France	5	13	16	12	10	weak	weak

Source: Hemerijck (1992).

The research gathered in this table had two objectives: to determine varying corporatist structures in capitalist democracies and to use these rankings to compare the economic performance of these countries. With respect to the latter objective the general supposition is that there is a significant influence of corporatist structures on economic outcomes.[35] However, serious criticism concerns the static nature of these rankings (see, for example, Scharpf, 1987; Woldendorp, 1995). As explained, corporatism may be seen as a structure or system of social, political and economic relations. In comparative research the relations between the actors (labour unions, political parties, employers' organizations) are, in a way, assumed to be constant or structurally determined. In consequence, there is little room for strategic choices by

---

[35] For a discussion of the empirical results of these comparative studies, see Wilke (1991a).

the actors and for changes of policy. Countries are in a given degree either corporatistically organized or they are not. No attention is paid to changing institutions, or, in the words of Wilke (1991a), institutional flexibility is neglected in this kind of research.

Further criticism concerns the differences in rankings. It seems as if subjective observation played a role in determining to what degree countries are characterized by corporatist structures. The rankings decisively determine the empirical results. It can therefore be asked how the variation in the rankings influence this type of research and how the various examinations may be compared. Obviously, the authors used different criteria for constructing their rankings, a variety of dependent variables, different periods and different data (Wilke, 1991a). In short, this type of research, examining the interaction between politics and economics, seems unsatisfactory. 'While the long debate on neo-corporatism has drawn attention to the potential significance of institutional strategies in policy making, attempts to force industrialized western countries into a one-dimensional neo-corporatism continuum have failed' (Korpi, 1991: 346).

Apart from corporatism, comparative political economics compares the partisan composition of governments to explain varying economic performances. Cameron (1978) reported for 18 countries (1960-1975) a significant correlation between the growth of the public economy (the role of the state) and the partisan composition of governments. He also examined the impact of electoral competition but found only a modest correlation between the frequency of elections and the increase of the public economy. From an examination of the same sample of countries (1965-1982) Cameron (1984) concluded that countries with relatively more frequent left control of the government performed better with regard to unemployment, and experienced, in contrast to the hypothesis of Hibbs (1977a), lower increases in the rate of inflation. These countries also experienced a lower amount of strikes. The same conclusions hold for the correlation of these economic variables and a measure for the organizational power of labour.

More work on the impact of parties is collected in a volume edited by Castles (1982a). Most examinations conclude that partisan control of government is a major determinant of policy. For example, Castles himself reported a correlation between right-wing incumbency and lower levels of public spending (Castles, 1982b; 18 OECD countries, early 1960s until mid 1970s). However, many authors at the same time tone down such a conclusion and point to a variety of interfering political factors of which the institutional environment is the most important. Van Arnhem and Schotsman (1982) concluded that labour unions are more important than parties with respect to income distribution. This conclusion is supported by Schmidt (1982), who explained that Social Democratic control of the government is only important if it is accompanied by a strong and united labour movement.[36] Thus with respect to economic performance there is a correlation between the institutional structure (corporatism) and the partisan composition of government.[37]

   To conclude, the examples of comparative political economics discussed in this section examine the influence of institutional structures and partisan governments on economic performance. Some research is focused on the institutional structure, notably on the way in which the labour movement is organized. Other research stresses the importance of the partisan composition of governments in relation to the institutional structure. Especially the role of Social Democratic, and sometimes Christian Democratic, parties is discussed. However, all this research in one way or another is very static. A country is corporatist or it is not. A country is dominated by Social Democratic parties or it is not. No attention is paid to strategic interaction between the various political actors. That means that no attention is paid to the political and economic

---

[36] With respect to the institutional limits for partisan impact on public policy Lehner and Schubert (1984) also referred to the importance of the bureaucracy which has to carry out the policy proposals of the politicians. The discussion about the relationship between politicians and bureaucrats was encouraged by economics of politics representative Niskanen (1971).

[37] Some recent papers following the road of comparative political research ought to be mentioned. All these papers employ pooled time series and cross sectional data to test the impact of institutional and political factors on economic performance empirically: Huber and Stephens (1993) on political parties and public pensions; Huber, Ragin and Stephens (1993) on Social Democracy, Christian Democracy and the constitutional structure and the welfare state; Blais, Blake and Dion (1993) on parties and the size of government; Hicks and Swank (1992) and Hicks and Misra (1993) on welfare spending in relation to political and institutional factors. Crepaz (1992) studied the influence of corporatism in especially the 1980s to react on the proposition that corporatism in the 1980s became less important. For a critical discussion of this line of research, see Amenta (1993).

circumstances determining the way in which economic policy is decided upon. In the following section strategic interaction is discussed.

Strategic Interaction in an Institutional Context

Whereas the models of political business cycles and the partisan theory appear to be too mechanistic, the analysis of comparative political economy focuses perhaps too much on institutional structures and neglects strategic interaction. However, there are some authors who try to combine both approaches - the politics of economics and the economics of politics - by examining the strategic interaction between political parties and labour organizations. Although he values the institutional approach to explaining the variance in economic performance of countries, Scharpf (1984) stressed the importance of strategic choice in economic policy. In his view the following three aspects have their influence: (i) institutional or structural factors such as corporatist structures or powerful labour movements; (ii) strategic choice, namely the choice political actors make with respect to priorities and means; and (iii) 'goodness of fit', as Scharpf named the importance of the appropriateness of strategies in different economic circumstances. Institutional factors are important, they can constrain economic policy, but neither the element of choice in economic policy should be neglected, nor the fact that a chosen strategy can fail because of prevailing economic circumstances.

In this section two different theories aiming at incorporating strategic interaction are compared. The first theory, the one of Garrett, Lange and others, is merely an extension of comparative political economics. It considers left-wing political parties and labour organizations as natural allies, but recognizes that the actions of both are interdependent. The second theory - Scharpf's model - uses a sort of game theoretical approach to look at the interaction between political actors (parties, unions, capital), and takes explicit account of the electoral consequences of various policies.

Garrett, Lange, and others: political interdependence In a comparative analysis of economic growth rates in 16 advanced capitalist democracies, Lange and Garrett (1985) criticized one of the implications of Olson's theory set out in his *Rise and Decline of Nations* (Olson, 1982). As an exception to his theory of collective action Olson argued that 'encompassing' unions, instead of just looking for their own gains, have an interest in favourable economic conditions for the country as a whole.[38] This argument strongly resembles the arguments of the politics of economics approach when referring to the relation between corporatist structures and macroeconomic performance. Lange and Garrett questioned Olson's implication. They argued that such a strategy (self regulation of labour organizations to promote higher economic growth) may lead to employers obtaining higher profits without sharing these with the unions. Although Olson has a point in stating that encompassing unions have an interest in promoting higher economic growth instead of only worrying about the distribution of national income, higher economic growth need not necessarily be distributed according to the wishes of encompassing unions.

In Olson's theory the choice between a strategy of collective gain or a distributional strategy depends on the relative group size. According to Lange and Garrett, however, the choice of strategy of the unions depends on political factors that diminish the risk of an unprofitable distribution of economic growth. For example, if the Left is politically strong in the government or in the electorate, unions will more likely follow a collective gain strategy. Hence there is a role for the state, for a governing left-wing political party, to play, namely to provide the circumstances in which encompassing unions are willing to cooperate and refrain from aggressive wage policies. In this situation, according to the authors, the state is also able to provide incentives for capital to invest in the economy. In other words, with respect to economic growth there is an advantageous cooperation between the state, labour organizations and capital because there is little uncertainty about the distribution of national product.

If either the political Left is weaker or the organization of labour is not encompassing, the conditions are less profitable. Moreover, in a situation where labour organizations are not encompassing it is unlikely that (the leaders of) labour unions are willing to choose a cooperative strategy, with or without left-wing government control. However, if labour is weakly organized and government control is in the hands of a

---

[38] Olson's fifth implication: 'encompassing organizations have some incentive to make the society in which they operate more prosperous, and an incentive to redistribute income to their members with as little excess burden as possible, and to cease such redistribution unless the amount redistributed is substantial in relation to the social cost of the redistribution' (Olson, 1982: 74).

right-wing political party there is a situation of free play for the market forces. Such a situation, which approximates a neo-classical world, is as advantageous for economic growth as the situation of a strong Left and encompassing unions.

The hypotheses were tested and confirmed with interaction models in which the independent political variables conditionally influence economic growth (capitalist democracies 1974-1980). Unlike earlier empirical research, in which either the organization of labour or the political strength of the Left acted as independent variables, it is now the interaction between these variables that (partly) explains differences in economic growth. It is worth mentioning here that control of the state by a left-wing party is more important than electoral strength. In political interaction it is not the strength measured in vote shares that is the most significant factor, but power in government.

Many contributions to comparative political economy seek to explain the divergent economic performance of capitalist democracies since the oil crisis of 1973 and the period of stagflation that followed. Garrett and Lange (1986) therefore tested the impact on economic growth of political relations as described above, while taking account of international economic relations. They not only tested the impact of political strategies but also took account of the size of the national markets, reliance on international trade and dependence on oil imports. They concluded that these factors certainly have their influence, but 'that politically rooted adjustment can significantly affect economic performance, even in the face of sharp changes in aggregate world demand and certain supply costs... that are beyond the reach of domestic politics' (Garrett and Lange, 1986: 544). The margins are not that narrow that national political strategies do not matter in 'a hostile world'.[39]

The research was taken a step further in Alvarez, Garrett and Lange (1991). In conformity with their earlier work, they hypothesized 'that there are two different paths to desirable macroeconomic performance. In countries with densely and centrally organized labour movements, leftist governments can promote economic growth and reduce inflation and unemployment. Conversely, in countries with weak labour movements, rightist governments can pursue their partisan-preferred macroeconomic strategies and achieve similarly beneficial macroeconomic

---

[39] For further evidence on the model of Lange and Garrett, see Hicks (1988) and Hicks and Patterson (1989).

outcomes' (Alvarez, Lange and Garrett, 1991: 539). As in much other modern comparative political economic research empirical analysis was performed by the method of pooled time series (16 advanced industrial democracies, 1967-1984). The hypothesis was verified for economic growth, inflation and unemployment. Although in a re-estimation of the model the results for unemployment and inflation were toned down (Beck, Katz, Alvarez, Garrett and Lange, 1993), political economic interaction remained an important explanation for differences in economic growth.

This discussion of the work by Garrett, Lange and others makes it clear that in order to make a distinction between the economic performance of countries with left-wing governments and right-wing governments the organization of labour, and the labour market, has to be taken into account. Strategic interaction between the political parties in the state sector and the institutional market forces appears to be an important element in explaining the impact of parties on economic outcomes. In addition, the impact of the strategic policy choices by organized labour depends on the party political power constitution. The two patterns of economic success described in this section show a striking resemblance with the labour relations characterized by Bruno and Sachs (1985) and Calmfors and Driffill (1988). Bruno and Sachs and Calmfors and Driffill recognized that the institutional context - the organization of the labour market - is an important factor in explaining divergent economic performance. However, Garrett and Lange and their collaborators showed, in addition, that the political constellation also influences the working of the labour market. Nevertheless, it is exaggerated to speak about strategic interaction. The theory of Garrett et al. considers the connection between the labour movement and a left-wing political party too much as a natural relation. The model of Scharpf demonstrates that a beneficial cooperation between labour and a left-wing government is dependent on the economic and political circumstances.

Scharpf: strategies in a combination of a coordination game and an electoral game Scharpf (1987, 1991) has developed an elegant framework to analyse comparatively the strategic macroeconomic policy choices of political actors in West Germany, Great Britain, Austria and Sweden since the economic crisis of the early 1970s. Before this period of stagflation these countries (and other OECD countries) were comparable regarding their economic performances as well as the political colour of their governments. Apart from having similar growth rates, and similar unemployment and inflation figures, these four countries were all governed around 1973 by left-wing political parties. However, after the oil crisis the economic performances of the four countries diverged. The question arises, why?

Unlike much political economic research Scharpf explicitly formulated the economic conditions under which political relations develop and policy choices are made. In a typology of economic problems of the 1970s he distinguished between two sources of inflation and unemployment: on the demand side there may be demand pull inflation and Keynesian unemployment, whereas on the supply side there may be cost push inflation and classical (profit gap) unemployment. Due to the rising prices of oil and the transfer of an enormous amount of money to the OPEC, there was, according to Scharpf, a combination of cost push inflation and Keynesian unemployment.

Referring to Tinbergen (1952), Scharpf explained that with two macroeconomic instruments, monetary policy (assuming that the central bank is part of national government) and fiscal policy, the government was not able to handle the two economic problems simultaneously, because both instruments work in the same direction: 'both could be used to reflate aggregate demand by increasing government expenditures or cutting taxes, and by increasing the money supply and lowering interest rates. Alternatively, both instruments could be used restrictively, by reducing the fiscal deficit and the money supply. As both sets of instruments affect the same parameters of aggregate demand, they needed to be employed in parallel in order to be effective. Under the conditions of stagflation, that meant that governments were able to fight either inflation or unemployment, but not both at the same time. Worse yet, in trying to solve one problem they would aggravate the other one' (Scharpf, 1987: 232).

The solution of this dilemma lies in the coordination of governmental economic policy and wage policy of the labour unions. According to Scharpf the direct effect wages have on the supply side is stronger than the effect on the demand side. Therefore, moderation of wage demands makes it possible for the government to use its instruments for Keynesian policies. Full employment can be promoted without the risk of runaway inflation. However, it depends on the objectives and strategies of the political actors for such a cooperation to take place.

The political actors are: the government (left-wing or right-wing), the central bank and the labour unions. Capital (organizations of employers) is not considered to be a political actor deciding on macroeconomic policy. So, if it is assumed that central bank policy is a component of total government policy, there are two possible *coordination games* between governments and unions: a Keynesian game and a monetarist game. At the same time there is the *political game* in which political parties consider the electoral consequences of chosen strategies and economic circumstances. Scharpf divided the various groups of voters - 'different groups of voters will respond differently to macro-economic strategies' (Scharpf, 1987: 241) - into three socio-economic strata: (i) the upper stratum, including rentiers/capitalists, managers/entrepreneurs and self-employed professionals; (ii) the middle stratum, including skilled blue and white collar workers and professionals; and (iii) the lower stratum of the unskilled workers, unemployed workers and welfare clients. The first stratum is considered to be the core constituency of a bourgeois or conservative political party and prefers monetarist policies. The third stratum prefers a labour government and Keynesian policies. The middle stratum plays a pivotal role. Its preferences and voting behaviour depend on the economic circumstances. The interaction between both games, the political game and the coordination game, leads to four possible situations. As Scharpf did in his article, these situations are explained one by one:

(i) *Keynesian government policies and moderate wage demands; low unemployment and moderate inflation* In the situation of union wage moderation a Labour government is able to pursue its partisan goal of full employment by Keynesian policies. The economic conditions would be favourable as well as the political consequences. The core constituency would be content with the situation and the middle stratum of voters would not have a reason to vote for a Conservative party at the next election. The voters of the upper stratum would be less content if its preferred Conservative government was in the situation of this Keynesian game. However, although the Conservative government would not be able to pursue its partisan goal it would not shift to a monetarist policy, because the middle group of voters is satisfied with the situation and the upper stratum of voters would not turn to the labour party. Accordingly, because of electoral consequences, a Conservative government would also stick to a Keynesian policy.

(ii) Keynesian government policies and agressive wage demands; low unemployment and very high inflation The situation would change if union wage policy became more aggressive. Scharpf claimed that labour unions are more concerned with real wages than with inflation, certainly if they believe to have enough market power to be able to compensate for inflation. If government policy remained expansive, full employment would be maintained while the unions demanded higher wages. For a Labour government this would be an alarming situation. With rising inflation the middle stratum of voters would shift its vote to a Conservative government. The switch to a monetarist policy would worsen the situation (very high unemployment, high inflation), unless the unions could be persuaded by such a policy to moderate wages again. With a monetarist policy and moderate unions the electoral position would be safe again. However, according to Scharpf, this would be gambling on the short term reaction of the labour unions. For a Conservative government the electoral position of a situation in which inflation rises due to an aggressive wage policy would not be so dangerous. It could stick to a Keynesian policy, knowing that the middle voter stratum would like something to be done about high inflation but would not entrust a Labour government with such a task.

(iii) Monetarist government policies and aggressive wage demands; very high unemployment and high inflation An economic situation with very high unemployment and high inflation would probably be electorally fatal for both types of governments. Furthermore, if such a situation persisted for some time it would be likely that the labour unions would shift their policy to a moderation of wage claims.

(iv) Monetarist government policies and moderate wage demands; high unemployment and low inflation The political implications of the economic situation with high unemployment and low inflation depend on the preceding situation. After experiencing a period of time of a Keynesian policy with low unemployment, the middle voter stratum would not be content with neither government shifting to a monetarist policy. Therefore, according to Scharpf, a rational government, unlike an independent central bank, would

not make such a policy shift. If, however, the foregoing period of time displayed the worst situation possible, the middle voter stratum would be content, for the time being, with an improvement of the situation by a monetarist policy. For a Conservative government it is even the best possible situation to be in. The middle group of voters would be reassured and the core constituency would be satisfied because of the pursuing of partisan goals (low inflation and, with restrained wage demands, higher profits). For a Labour government the situation would be more ambiguous. The improvement of the situation would satisfy the middle group of voters. However, the core constituency would rather have the Labour party reverting to a Keynesian policy.

These are the four possible situations of Scharpf's model. Scharpf used his model to explain the different policy choices and diverging economic performances in West Germany, Great Britain, Austria and Sweden during the 1970s. The theory was successful in explaining the shift of various governments from Keynesian to monetarist policies. Scharpf concluded by explaining that the neo-corporatist organization of labour is only of importance during a Keynesian game. In such a situation an encompassing labour movement is important to prevent inflation from rising by restraining wage demands. During a monetarist regime labour unions, encompassing or not, always have an incentive to refrain from aggressive wage policies. Free rider problems are in such a situation less important because of the danger of massive unemployment.

Lange and Garrett recognized that 'encompassing labour organisation is only positively associated with growth when accompanied by Left control of the government, and Left governments only have a positive impact on economic growth when labour is highly and centrally organised' (Lange and Garrett, 1985: 792). With this observation Lange and Garrett criticized the earlier (empirical) research on neo-corporatism and extended the arguments of Olson (1982) and Calmfors and Driffill (1988) with respect to the institutional features of countries, in emphasizing the importance of partisan politics and the strategic interaction between political parties and labour organizations. However, in their theory it is still the institutional structure which is important. It is the organization of labour in combination with, as it were, the organization of government that determines economic performance. This combination was a new element in the theory and empirical research on neo-corporatism, but it is an exaggeration to state that it is strategic interaction.

The difference between the interaction described by Lange, Garrett and collaborators and the interaction in the model of Scharpf is the difference in emphasis on the economic and political circumstances in which the actors interact. In the framework of Lange, Garrett and others the unions let their behaviour - aggressive or cooperative - depend on the political strength of the left-wing political party (does it have control of the government?). The political strength of the Left is not decisive in the model of Scharpf. On the contrary, unions let their actions depend on both the economic situation and on the policies of either type of government. Moreover, in a situation of low unemployment and a Keynesian Labour government labour unions even have an incentive to take an aggressive stand in wage negotiations. There is not an immediate danger of rising unemployment and unions may therefore demand higher wages. This possibility contradicts the theory of Lange and others. Unlike their theory, which perhaps too much considers the relation between left-wing parties and labour organizations as natural, Scharpf's model examines the interaction between these political actors depending on political and economic conditions.

1.5 Conclusion

A survey of the literature is always subjective and never complete. It is partly determined by purposeful choices and partly by coincidence. The choice of this chapter was to give a survey of both some models of political economic interaction and of some examples of the theories of the politics of economics. In this way it was intended to illustrate the limitations of political economic models by discussing comparative political economic research.

A wide variety of political economic theories were discussed. The chapter started with the political business cycle. In this theory the electoral goals of opportunistic politicians or political parties determine economic policy. Next, the theory of the partisan models was presented. Political parties not only have electoral objectives, they also have ideological goals. Both types of models are rather mechanistic. Therefore, the theories of the politics of economics or comparative political economics were discussed. These theories stress the importance of institutional structures in determining economic policies and outcomes. However, these theories tend to neglect the possiblity of political actors making policy choices dependent on economic and political circumstances. Finally, the model of Scharpf was presented as a combination of the politics of economics approach and the economics of politics approach.

Elster (1989) emphasized the importance of mechanisms rather than general laws in the social sciences. He argued that the social sciences can offer many mechanisms, and show their importance for behaviour, but that they cannot offer the necessary and sufficient conditions under which the various mechanisms are switched on: 'one cannot have a law to the effect that "if p, then sometimes q"' Elster (1989: 10). The central argument in the political business cycle models is a mechanism as described by Elster. Self-interested politicians may manipulate the economic instruments at their disposal in such a way that their chances of reelection are maximized. This mechanism can explain, for example, the economic policies by president Nixon in the United States in the 1970s. However, self-interest is not the only motive that makes governments decide on economic policy. Moreover, political, economic or other conditions may interfere with the initial purpose of governments to create a political business cycle. The theory of the political business cycle considers the relation between office-motivated politicians and their policies to be a general law. However, although the argument has an intuitive attraction and contributes to understanding social reality, it is not a law.

The same holds for the models of the partisan theory. Based on the exploitable Phillips curve these models describe the law of alternating governments and their distinct policies. Like the political business cycle theories it only considers a (possible) mechanism between political motivation and economic policies. In contrast, the politics of economics examines institutional structures, rather than mechanisms. It is institutional structures that determine the way in which economic policies are decided upon. Differences in institutional structures of countries are assumed to explain variations in economic performance. As explained in this chapter, the hypotheses of the politics of economics (comparative political economics) are tested empirically by constructing institutional variables. Measures for these variables are, for example, the degree of unionization, the centralization of labour unions, but also the degree of dominance, over a certain period of time, of left-wing political parties in government. In this kind of empirical research there is no room for political mechanisms. Consequently, this research neglects the possible mechanisms of the economics of politics.

In Scharpf's model the political motivations determining economic policy in the models of the political business cycle and the partisan theory are combined with the institutional factors of the corporatism debate. It is the economic and political circumstances that determine the way in which political actors make their policy choices. Thus the model of Scharpf is presented as a theoretical reaction to both the mechanistic political economic interaction models and the structuralistic approach of comparative political economics. Authors such as Scharpf and Lange, Garrett and others provided a starting-point in examining the interaction between political parties and labour organizations. The institutional framework in some circumstances may clearly constrain political parties in creating a political business cycle or in achieving partisan goals, but it may also enable parties, in other circumstances, to implement exactly those policies which are strategically most preferred. Important in Scharpf's model are the strategic policy choices politicians may make under varying conditions. However, because these conditions are not fixed, the problem is that it cannot be predicted when mechanisms will have a dominant influence on political economic outcomes, dominant in relation to institutional structures. The empirical investigation of Scharpf's model is, by necessity, more of a descriptive character than the investigations of both the mechanistic models of political economic interaction and the institutional theories of comparative political economics.

The subsequent chapters of this book investigate whether the political economic interaction models have empirical relevance for the Dutch economy. In chapter two the partisan theory is examined; in chapter three the political business cycle. The order of chapter one (first the political business cycle, then the partisan theory) is reversed to make some remarks about the Dutch political parties first. The objective of the examination of the interaction models is to establish the explanatory power of these mechanisms for Dutch political economic relations. In chapter four a general framework, inspired by Scharpf's model, is used to analyse political economic interaction in a more descriptive way. This analysis is meant to comment on the results of chapters two and three. In this way it is recognized that mechanisms may work, but that institutional arrangements and structural developments also play their part. In chapter four the characteristics of the so-called Dutch model are explained.

2 Partisan Politics in the Dutch Economy

2.1 Introduction

According to public opinion, politics matters only marginally in the Netherlands. It was the former Social Democratic Prime Minister Den Uyl who admitted that in the field of social economic policies the margins are narrow (Den Uyl, 1978). Due to the fact that governments are formed by a coalition of parties, policy is dominated by the concept of consensus, rather than by partisan goals. Moreover, consensus is found not only between political parties in government, it is also agreed upon by institutionally organized interests such as the labour movement and employers' organizations. Hierarchically organized the leaders of political parties and interest organizations decide on political matters. With respect to the formation of governments and formulating policies, De Swaan explained that after the general election, for which the leaders mobilized their constituencies with an appeal on loyalty, it is the leaders who, in a secretive way, do the bargaining and take the decisions. It is in this process that parties (or political leaders) wishing to take part in the government have to forego promises made before the election in election programmes (see De Swaan, 1982).[1]

Nevertheless, coalitions are formed by political parties that are perceived to differ ideologically. It is therefore relevant to examine whether political parties alternating in a coalition government make a difference. Moreover, taking the role of the confessional parties into account, with the Catholics taking part in government from 1918 until 1994, it is relevant to investigate whether it makes a difference whether the Social Democrats or the Conservative Liberals take part in government. This is done in the present chapter. The political role of the labour movement and employers' organizations and their interaction with the government is discussed in chapter four.

---

[1] For an illuminative characterization of the process of cabinet formation, see Stevens, Giebels and Maas (1994).

In the present chapter it is examined whether the partisan theory, as surveyed in chapter one, has empirical relevance for the Netherlands.[2] Does ideology affect the Dutch economy and, if so, are these effects in accordance with the partisan theory? In section two a brief anthology of election programmes is presented to get insight into the ideological differences between Dutch political parties. Subsequently, a few political or ideology variables are constructed to be able to test empirically whether the Dutch economy is affected by ideology. In section three macroeconomic outcomes are subjected to time-series examination. Economic policy variables are investigated in section four.

2.2 Political Parties and Ideology

In table 2.1 the post-war Dutch coalition governments are presented. The major political parties are the Social Democrats (PvdA), the Christian Democrats (CDA, originating from smaller confessional parties at the end of the 1970s (CHU, ARP, KVP)) and the Conservative Liberals (VVD). Sometimes smaller parties take part in the government as well, such as, for example, the Social Liberals (D66) in 1973, 1982 and 1994. For an explanation of all the abbreviations, see the list at the end of the book. For a somewhat more extensive description of the Dutch political system, see chapter four. For now it is sufficient to know when the PvdA or the VVD participated in the government.

Before the partisan models are subjected to a formal test, it is useful to cursorily analyse whether parties really differ from each other ideologically and whether partisan goals diverge substantially. Political scientists stress the importance of election programmes for political parties. Pennings and Keman mentioned two aspects: firstly, the accomplishment of a programme is a long process with all sorts of participation procedures for the constituency. It, therefore, has to be taken seriously by the party leaders. Moreover, Demsetz argued, the organization of a political party depends on its active constituency. Active party members are member of a political party because of its political ideology. Therefore, political leaders have to take account of the election programme that is an ideological product of the party as an organization (Demsetz, 1990). Secondly, election programmes are a strategic

---

[2] Parts of this chapter were already published in Snels (1995a).

instrument during elections and during government formations. For example, it is the election programmes which form the starting point for negotiations to form a new coalition government (Pennings and Keman, 1993).

Table 2.1   Governments in the Netherlands, 1952-1998

Period	Cabinet	Parties
1956-1958	Drees III	CHU, KVP, ARP, PvdA
1958-1959	Beel ll	CHU, KVP, ARP
1959-1963	De Quay	CHU, KVP, ARP, VVD
1963-1965	Marijnen	CHU, KVP, ARP, VVD
1965-1966	Cals	ARP, KVP, PvdA
1966-1967	Zijlstra	ARP, KVP
1967-1971	De Jong	CHU, KVP, ARP, VVD
1971-1972	Biesheuvel I	CHU, KVP, ARP, VVD, DS'70
1972-1973	Biesheuvel II	CHU, KVP, ARP, VVD
1973-1977	Den Uyl	ARP, KVP, PvdA, PPR, D66
1977-1981	Van Agt I	CDA, VVD
1981-1982	Van Agt II	CDA, PvdA, D66
1982-1982	Van Agt III	CDA, D66
1982-1986	Lubbers I	CDA, VVD
1986-1989	Lubbers II	CDA, VVD
1989-1994	Lubbers/Kok	CDA, PvdA
1994-1998	Kok	PvdA, D66, VVD

Source: CBS.

Partisan goals are not a constant factor. They change over time as a function of political, economic and cultural changes. However, there are differences of opinion, even ideological differences, with respect to the role of the state, public finance, income distribution and so forth. A brief anthology of past election programmes, going backwards in time, confirms this notion. In 1989, after two consecutive cabinets with the Christian Democrats and the Conservative Liberals, the Social Democrats wrote in their programme: 'the confidence in the working of the market is exaggerated at the expense of the attention to the quality of the functioning, services and responsibilities of the government' (Lipschits, 1989: 233, original in Dutch).[3] And: 'the aim is to improve the

---

[3] 'Het vertrouwen in de werking van de markt is doorgeschoten ten koste van de aandacht voor de kwaliteit van functioneren, dienstverlening en

purchasing power of the lowest income groups more than that of the higher income groups' (Lipschits, 1989: 236).[4] At the same time the Christian Democrats stressed the importance of the own responsibility of the individual, a centerpart of their ideology, and defended the policy changes with respect to the welfare state: 'a transitional period is initiated. Transition from an overburdened welfare state, with a considerable role for the government and a constantly growing collective sector, towards a type of a social constitutional state and a society, with more responsibilities for citizens and organizations and a government concentrating on its essential tasks' (Lipschits, 1989: 380).[5]

In 1989 the tone of the election programmes of the Christian Democrats and of the Social Democrats seemed moderate, almost as if they were explicitly written for a possible coalition between the two parties. In contrast, in 1986 the programme of the Social Democrats contained phrases that seemed much more radical, for example with respect to incomes policy: 'policy should be aimed at a net income proportion of 1:3, and the very high incomes should be limited first' (Lipschits, 1986: 319).[6] The difference with the Conservative Liberals is obvious: 'since a long time incomes policy has been aimed at levelling of incomes. In the future a greater significance should be given to the benefit of income differences in stimulating economic growth' (Lipschits, 1986: 448).[7]

---

verantwoordelijkheden van de overheid.'

[4] 'Er wordt naar gestreefd de koopkracht van de laagste inkomensgroepen gunstiger te doen ontwikkelen dan die van de hogere inkomensgroepen.'

[5] 'Een overgangsperiode is ingezet. Overgang van een overbelaste verzorgingsstaat, met een aanzienlijke overheidsrol en een voortdurend groeiende collectieve sector, naar een type sociale rechtsstaat en een samenleving, met meer verantwoordelijkheden voor burgers en organisaties en met een overheid die zich sterker profileert op haar wezenlijke taken.'

[6] 'Het beleid dient er op gericht te zijn een netto-inkomensverhouding van 1:3 dichterbij te brengen, waarbij de zeer hoge inkomens het eerst moeten worden verlaagd.'

[7] 'Het inkomensbeleid is gedurende een lange periode in overwegende mate gericht geweest op nivellering van inkomens. In de toekomst dient het beleid een

The idea of a crisis of the welfare state and the notion that the public finance situation was unsound were formed at the end of the 1970s and the beginning of the 1980s. In 1981 the Christian Democrats wrote: 'sooner or later the unpaid bills are presented', and: 'the social security system is in danger', moreover: 'we commit excessive exploitation by making the incomes of the active and inactive working population increase at the expense of the posibilities of businesses to invest' (Lipschits, 1981: 10).[8] Four years earlier the Social Democrats thought to continue their participation (with even a leading role) in the government: 'four years is not enough. We want to go forwards. Forwards on the road of fair distribution. Four years is not enough to bring inequality between people to an end. Redistribution of income, knowledge, power and employment; democratization on all fields, takes a long battle against vested interests' (Lipschits, 1977: 163).[9]

The picture of partisan differences regarding income distribution, the role of the state and public finance is also confirmed by comparison of earlier election programmes. It follows from a comparison of the election programmes of 1971 that partisan differences were concentrated on the growth and the direction of public expenditures (De Bruyn, 1971). The confessional parties and the Social Democrats advocated a stronger growth of public expenditures than the Conservative Liberals. The policy position of the PvdA about the use of the growth of national income was determined by a report written in 1963: *Om de kwaliteit van het bestaan* (Wiardi Beckmanstichting, 1963). With respect to welfare policy the Social Democrats stressed the importance of public expenditures. The 1960s were characterized by continuous economic growth. For this

---

grotere betekenis toe te kennen aan het nut van inkomensverschillen ter bevordering van de economische groei.'

[8] 'Vroeg of laat worden de onbetaalde rekeningen gepresenteerd.' 'Het stelsel van sociale zekerheid loopt gevaar.' 'Wij plegen roofbouw door de inkomens van actieven en inactieven te laten groeien ten koste van de mogelijkheden om in de bedrijven te investeren.'

[9] 'Vier jaar is niet genoeg. Wij willen voorwaarts. Voorwaarts op de weg van Eerlijk Delen. Vier jaar is niet voldoende om aan de ongelijkheid tussen mensen een einde te maken. Herverdelen van inkomen, kennis, macht en arbeid; democratisering op alle terreinen, betekent een jarenlange strijd tegen gevestigde belangen.'

reason, the political debate was dominated by welfare political issues and income distribution. The PvdA and the VVD had different ideas regarding incomes policy. For example, the PvdA, in contrast to the VVD, wanted to use tax policy to redistribute income.

Hoogerwerf (1963) compared the election programmes of 1948 and 1963. Immediately after World War II the PvdA took a radical point of view regarding social economic policy. Economic planning was a central point of Social Democratic ideology. Socialization of large parts of the industry and equalization of incomes were important aspects of PvdA policy proposals. In 1963 the PvdA already moderated its ideas about socialization. However, Hoogerwerf maintained that, although the PvdA and the VVD were converging with respect to socialization and planning ideas, the opinions about income and wealth distribution remained signifcantly divergent.

This is only a cursory anthology and discussion of the election programmes of the main political parties in the Netherlands. Some insight is given into the ideological views of these parties. The election programmes hint at persisting differences in ideology and policy goals. However, it is also clear that partisan ideology is not fixed, but changes over time. Consequently, the measure of polarization between the political parties may oscillate. This could have its effects on economic policies. Still, irrespective of the fact that ideology changes, the question remains whether partisan ideology affects economic policy and economic outcomes at all.

In 1995 Van Dalen and Swank published research results indicating an ideological effect in various categories of government spending. Observing that in the Netherlands only little research has been done on the impact of politics on government spending, Van Dalen and Swank examined various categories of spending: spending on defense, infrastructure, public administration, education, health care and social security. They concluded that especially spending on public administration, health care and social security is positively correlated with the political colour of the government: left-wing governments raise spending, whereas right-wing governments cut back on these categories of government spending.

Spending on health care programmes and social security (transfers) probably have the strongest effects on the income distribution. It is, therefore, not surprising that these expenditures are the ones demonstrating the most significant indications of being politically motivated. In Van Wijck (1989, 1990, 1991a and b) and Van Wijck and Arts (1991) various models of the political impact on the income distribution were tested. However, in the Netherlands there is a lack of data regarding the income distribution. Various indicators were used in these publications: the Theil coefficient (1958-1985, with rather many data points missing), income shares of deciles (1959-1985), and the amount of net old age benefits (AOW) compared to average net income (1959-1988). Most of the empirical tests reported, initially demonstrated a significant political influence. However, Van Wijck (1991a) put these results in perspective by, among other things, considering the influences of business cycles and demographical developments. The significance of the political impact considerably diminished. Apparently, it is not easy to clearly alter the income distribution in the desired direction. Anyhow, it is an important variable for political economic interaction. Van Wijck quoted Alesina about the partisan theory: 'the basic idea is that politics is about income distribution' (Van Wijck, 1991b: 306, Alesina, 1989: 60). Unfortunately, the lack of data complicates research. Therefore, instead of testing the partisan theory on the basis of income distribution variables, other macroeconomic and policy variables are examined in this chapter.

To be able to test the partisan theory, which is the purpose of the present chapter, it is necessary to construct an ideology variable. A number of variables are used in this chapter. Usually the partisan theory assumes a political system with two political parties and, therefore, two possible governments: a left-wing one and a right-wing one (a Democratic or a Republican president in the United States, a Labour or a Conservative government in the United Kingdom). For empirical tests of the partisan theory in two-party-democracies usually a binary variable is used. In the Netherlands it is not satisfactory to make such a simple bipartite division. As there are only coalition governments in the Netherlands it is obvious to at least take account of the divison of power between the coalition partners. Therefore, instead of using a binary variable, a variable is used that takes account of the number of left and right-wing ministers in the government. This variable was constructed by Van Dalen and Swank (1996, 1995a and b). Henceforth this variable is named MINISTER.[10]

---

[10] The political variable of Van Dalen en Swank: $(M_l-M_r)/(M_l+M_c+Mr)$. M_l is the number of left-wing ministers (PvdA, D66, DS'70), M_c is the number of ministers from the political centre (CDA (KVP,ARP,CHU)) and M_r is the number

The way in which ideology is modelled in political economic research - binary variables, but also the variable MINISTER - does not take account of strategic considerations or changing views of political parties.[11] Governments are either left-wing or right-wing governments, and this fact only is to have systematic influence on economic variables. In this way the partisan theory predicts automatic and mechanistic developments. A change of governments determines a change in economic policies. There are only a few examples of research trying to take account of complicating factors.

One example is the approach of Frey and Schneider (1978a and b). By combining ideological preferences with opinion poll data this research is a combination of political business cycle and partisan theory. Another example is the model of Hibbs (1994). Reacting on the partisan theory with rational expectations, Hibbs took account of the prevailing economic situation influencing partisan policies. In his view parties learn about the inflationary consequences of their expansionary economic policies and may, therefore, temper their ideological goals. Both the models of Frey and Schneider and Hibbs try to take account of strategic considerations of partisan governments. Both models acknowledge that left-wing governments do not automatically stimulate economic growth to boost employment. Both models stress the importance of an extra factor playing

---

of right-wing ministers (VVD). The variable MINISTER in this book uses, in contrast to Van Dalen and Swank, in the transitional years the weighted average of the value of the two governments involved. The weight is determined by the number of months of both governments in transitional years. In other words, there is a small difference between the variable MINISTER and the original variable of Van Dalen and Swank.

[11] A factor also neglected is the importance of Christian Democratic parties. Christian Democrats are perceived to be in the centre of the political spectrum. It is the participation of either the Social Democrats or the Conservative Liberals deciding whether a government is a left-wing or a right-wing government. This binary distinction is the only distinction that is of importance for partisan theory. This is a simplistic assumption. See, for example, Esping-Andersen (1990) and Van Kersbergen (1995) for the special role Catholic parties in particular, and Christian Democrats in general, have had on social economic policies.

a role, namely popularity and inflation. However, both models remain highly mechanistic, despite these modifications.[12]

Economic models are, by definition, a simplification of reality. In chapter four a general framework is used to describe the role of political parties as well as labour unions and employers' organizations in formulating economic policies. However, in the present chapter the purpose is to test the partisan theory. To take account of the aforementioned criticism, an alternative approach is used in modelling ideology. Instead of using binary ideology variables, a variable based on political science research is used for the empirical tests. This variable takes account of the fact that ideological preferences of political parties are not constant. Recent research programmes of political scientists are formulated to analyse the (developments in the) contents of election programmes (and other political documents). The aim of the analysis is to determine whether it is possible to place political parties on a left to right scale and to analyse longitudinal developments of partisan goals. Pennings and Keman systematically investigated the party differences in the Netherlands. They came to the conclusion that there are significant ideological differences between parties, accounting for differences in, for example, economic goals (Pennings and Keman, 1993; see also Michels, 1993). Pennings and Keman developed a left to right scale for the Netherlands based on election programmes (1946-1989). They also constructed such a scale on the basis of government programmes (*regeerakkoorden*).[13] The latter scale is used as an indicator of the

---

[12] One approach worth mentioning is the interest function approach initiated by Van Winden (1983) and further developed by Van Velthoven (1988) and Renaud (1989). According to this approach government behaviour is explained by the relative power positions of interest groups (for example, government sector employees, private sector employees, capital owners and dependants on transfer payments). One way of defining power is the relative size of pressure groups. Consequently, the changing size of pressure groups determines changing political goals. In stressing the importance of interest groups this approach resembles the theory of Becker (1983).

[13] The scale is developed in three steps. First, the scale of Castles and Mair (1984) is used. They made a classification (left, middle, right) based on judgements by 'experts' (political scientists). This classification is independent of election programmes. Second, use is made of an international research project (Comparative Manifestos Project) which scores election programmes of 24 countries for the

ideological perspective of governments. Because election programmes and government programmes change over time, it is plausible that the scale is influenced by economic, social and political circumstances. In this way it takes account of changing goals of political parties. This scale of Pennings and Keman is used in the next section as an ideology variable to test the partisan theory. Henceforth this variable is designated GOVERNM.

Finally, a constructed variable named AVERAGE is used. This construction takes the average value of the variables MINISTER and GOVERNM. In this way this variable measures the influence of the composition of governments and the influence of changing government ideology simultaneously. Thus, this variable assumes that the distribution of power together with ideology affects economic variables. Note, however, that power relations also play a role in formulating government programmes, next to ideological differences. So, AVERAGE really measures power distribution twice. In figure 2.1 the ideology variables are portrayed. The larger the value of the variables, the more the government is a left-wing government; the smaller the value of the variables, the more the government is a right-wing government.

In addition to these three variables, in the next section the exercises with variables constructed to test the rational expectations variant of the partisan theory are reported. As explained in part A, these models expect that left-wing governments bring about real economic effects only at the beginning of their government period. Only at the beginning of left-wing governments these models expect extra economic growth and employment. This transitory effect is caused by the uncertainty of the election outcome. In rational expectations models only unexpected shocks

---

number of sentences on 54 categories. These categories are constant over time. Then the scale of Castles and Mair is related to these issues and by way of correlation (with a definition of statistical limits) an issue is defined as typical left or right wing. Third, for every election year the left-to-right position of every party is computed: summarized emphasis on left-wing issues minus the summarized emphasis on right-wing issues. The theoretical maxima are 100, with emphasis completely on left-wing issues and -100, with emphasis completely on right-wing issues. Consequently, the zero score is the middle road of the political landscape. (In figure 2.1 the theoretical maxima are 1 and -1 to be able to compare them with MINISTER.) Pennings and Keman used the same scaling method for government programmes (*regeerakkoorden*). Note that this scale neglects the transitional cabinets Biesheuvel II (1972-1973) and Van Agt III (1982).

have real economic effects. The traditional partisan theory, in contrast, expects more employment and economic growth during the entire left-wing government term. For both types of models the expectation regarding inflation is the same: it is higher for the entire left-wing term.

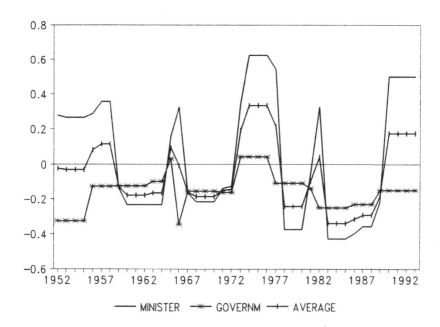

Figure 2.1 Ideology variables

To test the partisan models with rational expectations, a binary variable is used - RAT.EXP - taking the value one in the first two years of governments with the Social Democrats, and zero otherwise.[14] These exercises are executed to examine whether there are empirical indications of the partisan models with rational expectations. The period of time of two years is arbitrarily chosen. Alesina and Roubini (1992) tested a number of variants and found the best results for a variable referring to the first six quarters of left-wing government. Because in this book only yearly data are used, the period of two years was chosen. The exercises

---

[14] To check the results a variable is used taking the value one in later years of these governments, and zero otherwise.

in the next two sections are not meant to provide conclusive evidence for the hypothesis of rational expectations. The objective is to examine whether there is an ideological effect in the Dutch data, irrespective of whether these effects are durable for entire government periods or transitory and just observable at the beginning of left-wing governments' terms of office.

Since Hibbs (1977b) it has been standard practice to use the method of Box and Jenkins (1970) and Box and Tiao (1975) to estimate the impact of political factors on economic variables. The method is used to estimate the impact of an intervention term applied to a stochastic time series. The advantage of this method is that no structural model, describing causal relations, is necessary. It is assumed that a time series can be described by an ARIMA(p,d,q) model. Following Hibbs (1977b) to explain this method, a time series is assumed to be a stochastic white noise process of order p, d, q. The time series is differenced d times; the autoregressive-moving average process (ARMA) is defined by p lagged autoregressive terms and q moving average elements. Apart from the intervention variable - the political variables - the time series is assumed to be reflected by its own values of the past and a weighted average of current and lagged stochastic disturbances. Consequently, Box-Jenkins-Tiao models are partly a theoretical explanation and partly an artificial or theoretically unexplained description of stochastic time series. The weakness of this method is the lack of theory for the ARIMA specifications: there is no theoretical explanation for these specifications. It is only attempted to use the best ARIMA model according to statistical measures.

It is not only possible to criticize the theoretical underpinnings of the partisan theory, it is also clear that the empirical method has its shortcomings: (i) the construction of the political variables is decisive for the results. These variables contain arbitrary elements; (ii) moreover, there are only a few·data on which these variables are based: there are only a small number of cabinets with the Social Democrats; and (iii) with the help of econometric methods the correlation between political and economic variables is examined, but the dimensions of these variables are actually incomparable. A quantitative measurement of ideological effects is, therefore, hazardous. Although it is intuitively clear that ideology affects economic policy, it is difficult to determine the role of ideology by testing the rather simple hypotheses of the partisan theory with the help of econometric time-series analysis. Maybe the following citation of Orcutt is in place: 'doing econometrics is like trying to learn the laws of electricity by playing the radio' (cited in Leamer, 1983: 31). Nevertheless, in the two following sections econometric methods are used to test the models of the partisan theory for the Netherlands.

2.3 Macroeconomic Outcomes

The first empirical exercises concern the macroeconomic variables growth of national income, unemployment and inflation. These are the variables that traditionally play the leading part in political economic models. In section four the variables concerning economic policy are examined.[15]

Growth of Real National Income

To start with, the growth of real national income (RNI) is subjected to time-series analysis. In figure 2.2 the growth figures of national income are depicted together with the variable AVERAGE (the original value was multiplied by ten to facilitate optical comparison). This figure hints at a negative correlation between these two variables. A negative correlation, however, contradicts the partisan theory, for the original model of Hibbs (1977a) assumes left-wing governments to pursue growth stimulating policies.

Table 2.2 presents in four columns four models for the growth of national income. These models are estimated with the help of the Box-Jenkins-Tiao method. To save space, the coefficients and t-values of the autoregressive and moving-average components are left out. The order of the ARIMA model is presented at the top of the table (number of autoregressive components, number of times the time series is differenced, number of moving-average shocks). Furthermore, the coefficients and t-values of the ideology variables are presented, as well as the data indicating the statistical adequacy of the model. Notably the value of the Q statistic is of importance, because it is a measure of the probability that the residuals really are white noise (see Pindyck and Rubinfeld, 1991). In the process of testing various ARIMA models the

---

[15] At the time the empirical investigations were executed reliable time-series data were available until the beginning of the 1990s. In chapter four the data are updated until 1998.

purpose is to find the one with the lowest possible value of Q (with a significance level as high as possible, higher than, at least, 0.90).[16]

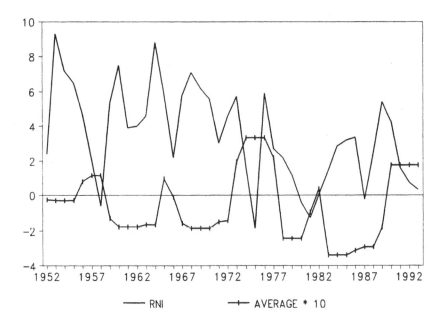

Figure 2.2 The growth of real national income and the ideology variable AVERAGE

The first two models in table 2.2 only estimate the correlation between national income and ideology (the variables AVERAGE and MINISTER). Both variables have statistically significant coefficients (at the 5% level). They are negatively correlated with the growth of national income. This result contradicts the expectations of the partisan theory.

---

[16] The modelling process implies that a decision is made as to how many times the time series is differenced to make it homogeneous. For the degree of differencing and for the orders of the moving average and autoregressive parts of the model the autocorrelation functions may be of assistance. The Q-value and the parameter estimates provide indications for the reliability of the estimates (see Pindyck and Rubinfeld, 1991). The t-values of the coefficients of the political variables should be significant at the 5% level. Sometimes results are reported with a significance level of 10%.

Table 2.2 Real national income (RNI)

	1	2	3	4
ARIMA	(0,1,4)	(0,1,4)	(2,1,2)	(2,1,2)
constant	-0.21	-0.06	-0.24	-0.14
	(-1.79)	(-0.46)	(-2.29)	(-1.74)
AVERAGE	-2.07		-1.63	
	(-3.52)		(-1.81)	
MINISTER		-1.14		-1.03
		(-2.60)		(-2.00)
DWORLD			0.32	0.32
			(5.22)	(5.67)
Q	10.17	9.35	6.39	6.56
(signif.)	(0.93)	(0.95)	(0.99)	(0.99)
DW	1.70	1.72	2.10	2.18
R^2	0.34	0.31	0.74	0.75

RNI: real national income, annual mutation in %, 1952-1993 (CPB)
DWORLD = WORLD(t)-WORLD(t-1); WORLD: annual mutation in % of weighted world trade, 1952-1993 (CPB)

Not reported in the table are the following exercises. An ARIMA(0,1,4) model is not suitable for the variable GOVERNM; the value for Q is too high. A model of much higher order (4,1,8) is acceptable, but in such a model the coefficient of GOVERNM is no longer significant. This means that no correlation was found between the variable constructed on the basis of government programmes and national income. Neither a significant correlation was found for the models testing the rational expectations hypothesis. The variable RAT.EXP was not significant, whereas the variable referring to later years of left-wing governments (the inverse of RAT.EXP) was significant at the 10% level. In other words, there are no clear indications in favour of the partisan theory with rational expectations. There was no extra growth of national income found in the early years of left-wing governments.

The Dutch economy is small and open. It, therefore, seems obvious to explicitly take account of international economic developments. In the time-series models 3 and 4 the variable WORLD - growth of world trade - is inserted as a seperate variable. The results demonstrate that the coefficients of the ideology variables are now significant at only the 10% level. GOVERNM (not reported) again was not significant; neither was RAT.EXP. The variable referring to the remaining years of left-wing governments was significant at the 5% level (t-value -2.07; negative correlation). Thus, there are no indications for extra growth in the early years of left-wing government periods, but there are signs of lower growth rates in subsequent years.[17]

Although inserting the variable WORLD diminishes statistical significance, figure 2.2 and the reported exercises hint at a negative correlation between the ideology variables and national income. This correlation is the opposite of the correlation expected by the partisan models. For the variable GOVERNM no correlation was found. Not a bit of evidence was found for the partisan theory with rational expectations.[18]

Unemployment

Unemployment is possibly the most important variable in the partisan theory. The assumption is that unemployment especially affects the voters of left-wing, Social Democratic parties. Therefore, the partisan theory expects employment stimulating policies from left-wing governments. According to the theory incorporating rational expectations, real effects of such policies are transitory and only visible at the beginning of left-wing

---

[17] Note, however, that this result is based on a few data only. There are few cabinets with the PvdA lasting longer than two years.

[18] Van Wijck (1997) tested both the partisan theory and the rational expectations partisan theory for economic growth in the Netherlands. Using an AR(7) model, and taking account of economic growth in Germany, he only found evidence for the partisan theory. He noted that other specifications, like the AR(2) specification used by Alesina and Roubini (1992), and other variables for international economic growth, like OECD growth instead of German economic growth, may lead to different outcomes. Different data and the use of ARIMA specifications in this book may explain why here, in contrast to Van Wijck, no evidence was found for additional economic growth with left-wing governments.

government terms. In this section various time series are examined. CPB data are used because these data form the longest time series. OECD data are used to compare Dutch unemployment data with European data. Table 2.3 presents the main results of the various exercises.

Table 2.3   Unemployment and employment in the market sector

	1 UR	2 UR	3 UR	4 UR	5 URNL	6 URNL	7 EMPL
ARIMA	(4,1,0)	(4,1,0)	(0,2,6)	(0,2,6)	(4,1,0)	(4,1,0)	(1,1,2)
constant	0.23	0.34					-0.05
	(0.65)	(1.00)					(-0.62)
MINISTER	1.25		1.06		0.62		-1.02
	(1.59)		(3.33)		(1.83)		(-2.05)
RAT.EXP		-0.74					
		(-1.31)					
AVERAGE				0.96		1.00	
				(2.45)		(2.05)	
DUREC					0.98	1.06	
					(7.08)	(6.50)	
Q	9.87	6.50	8.73	8.15	7.29	7.84	10.52
(signif.)	(0.94)	(0.99)	(0.97)	(0.98)	(0.95)	(0.93)	(0.91)
DW	2.07	2.02	1.97	1.85	1.82	1.80	1.83
R^2	0.95	0.95	0.95	0.95	0.98	0.98	0.59

UR: unemployment in % of dependent occupational population, 1952-1992 (CPB)
URNL: standard unemployment rate in % for the Netherlands, 1964-1993 (OECD)
DUREC = UREC(t)-UREC(t-1); UREC: standard unemployment rate in % for 12 countries of the European Community, 1964-1993 (OECD)
EMPL: volume change in employment market sector, 1952-1992 (CPB)

There were no ARIMA(x,1,x) models found with significant coefficients for the political variables. This may be explained by unemployment being non-stationary. Only MINISTER in model 1, in table 2.3, approaches the 10% significance level. Although not significant, it is remarkable that the variable RAT.EXP is the only variant with a negative coefficient, the sign expected by the (rational) partisan theory (model 2). The models 3 and 4 show the results of ARIMA(0,2,6) specifications. The ideology variables MINISTER and AVERAGE now have significant coefficients (at, respectively, the 1% and 5% level). They are positively correlated with unemployment. For GOVERNM no reliable results were found.

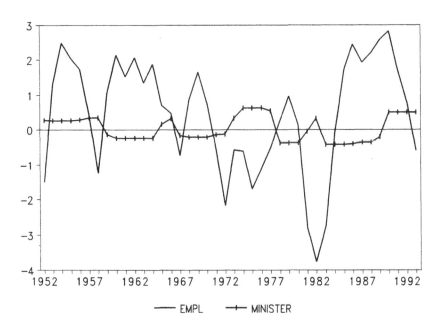

Figure 2.3 Volume change of employment in the market sector and the ideology variable MINISTER

Models 5 and 6 use OECD data to explicitly take account of the international dependency of the Dutch economy. The development of Dutch unemployment to a high degree resembles the development of European unemployment. Yet, there is a significant ideological influence: AVERAGE is significant at the 5% level, MINISTER only at the 10% level. Both variables are positively correlated with unemployment. Again, this is in contradiction with the partisan theory. Unemployment seems to increase with left-wing governments, even if international economic developments are taken into account. Neither for GOVERNM, nor for

RAT.EXP were significant results found. No evidence was found for the partisan theory with rational expectations.

Finally, model 7 takes some more distance from the partisan theory by examining the correlation between growth of employment in the market sector and partisan ideology. Figure 2.3 hints at a negative correlation between these variables. This optical conjecture is confirmed by time-series analysis. Model 7 demonstrates a significant negative correlation between employment in the market sector and the variable MINISTER (for GOVERNM and AVERAGE comparable correlations were found). This result is again in contradiction with the expectation that left-wing governments boost employment.[19]

Inflation

Inflation is the last macroeconomic variable examined. In all variants of the partisan theory inflation is expected to rise with left-wing governments. It is assumed that left-wing governments do not give priority to fighting inflation. It will rise as a consequence of Keynesian demand management policies to boost employment. The models incorporating rational expectations also expect inflation to rise with left-wing governments, because a low inflation goal would not be credible.

Figure 2.4 shows the development of the inflation rate and the ideology variable AVERAGE (multiplied by 10 for optical convenience). The exercises reported in table 2.4 seem to confirm the optical conjecture of a positive correlation between ideology and inflation. Except for GOVERNM (not in the table) ARIMA(x,0,x) specifications seem to give reliable results.[20] Both political variables, MINISTER and AVERAGE, are significant at the 5% level (models 1 and 2). In models 3 and 4 European inflation is inserted as a seperate variable. For these models an ARMA(2,6) specification seems suitable, although the value for Q barely

---

[19] To examine whether left-wing governments perhaps try to boost employment through the public sector, exercises using the variable volume change of employment in the public sector were performed. These exercises did not lead to results.

[20] The danger of this specification is that the results are affected by trend correlation.

reaches the 90% limit. AVERAGE is now significant at the 1% level; MINISTER at only 10%.

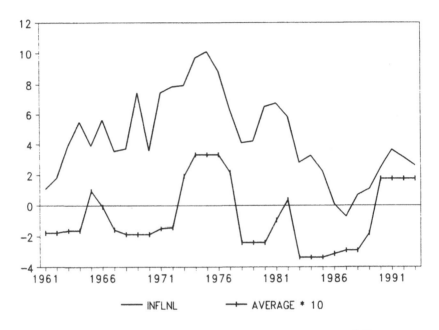

Figure 2.4 Inflation and the ideology variable AVERAGE

Figure 2.4 and the empirical exercises point at a positive correlation between inflation and left-wing ideology.[21] This correlation is in accordance with the partisan theory, be it that higher inflation is expected

---

[21] This result is in accordance with earlier research by Keizer (1982), who investigated the relation between inflation and ideology in the Netherlands. Keizer calculated an ideology indicator on basis of yearly policy statements of political actors. For political parties he analysed the contents of the yearly general political and financial speeches by the political leaders in parliament (*Algemene politieke en financiële beschouwingen*) with respect to income distribution, role of the market, and so forth. Using yearly policy documents a similar approach was used for labour unions and employers' organizations. Keizer found that his calculated measure explained a significant part of inflation during the period 1954-1978. Contrary to Keizer, De Grauwe (1985), using a simple test, did not find evidence for an ideological effect on inflation (nor for unemployment).

because of growth stimulating policies to reduce unemployment. However, the previous exercises showed no sign of extra economic growth or employment with left-wing governments. These results question the assumed Phillips curve trade-off between inflation and unemployment. Both inflation and unemployment seem to increase during left-wing government terms, even if international economic developments are taken into account.

Table 2.4   Inflation (INFLNL)

	1	2	3	4
ARIMA	(2,0,4)	(2,0,4)	(2,0,6)	(2,0,6)
MINISTER	2.50		1.69	
	(2.24)		(1.99)	
AVERAGE		5.98		4.46
		(2.96)		(3.71)
INFLEC			0.57	0.39
			(3.43)	(4.23)
Q	6.99	5.96	8.65	8.41
(signif.)	(0.96)	(0.98)	(0.90)	(0.91)
DW	1.76	1.88	1.79	2.00
R^2	0.76	0.79	0.87	0.92

INFLNL: yearly change consumer price index in % for the Netherlands, 1961-1993 (OECD)
INFLEC: idem for 12 countries of the European Community, 1962-1993 (OECD)

To conclude this section, it is remarkable that the variables MINISTER and AVERAGE demonstrate significant correlations, whereas GOVERNM, based on government programmes, does not seem to be correlated with macroeconomic outcomes (volume change of employment in the market sector (EMPL) is the only exception). According to the empirical analyses the content of government programmes only plays a role through the constructed variable AVERAGE.

2.4 Economic Policy

If governments pursue ideological goals, this should be visible, above all, in the instruments of economic policy. It may be difficult for governments to influence economic outcomes, they will certainly try to manipulate the instruments at their disposal (see also Tufte, 1978). In this section the correlation between the ideology variable and some policy variables are examined. Especially spending behaviour of governments is subjected to empirical analysis. Total government spending is examined, and, subsequently, social security spending.

Total government spending is an instrument of expansionary economic policies. Extra government spending leads to more employment, according to the Keynesian Phillips curve. According to the partisan models, left-wing governments are, therefore, expected to spend more than right-wing governments. Social security spending is investigated in order to establish whether or not left-wing governments are more generous regarding social security policies, than right-wing governments. These empirical tests take some more distance from the theoretical macroeconomic models.

Total Government Spending

In table 2.5 the results of the models estimating the correlation between government spending and GOVERNM are reported. Models with the other two ideology variables did not lead to satisfying results. Three models are estimated. In the first model, with only an ideology variable, GOVERNM has a significant coefficient at the 5% level. There is a positive correlation between government spending and the content of government programmes. The second model explicitly takes account of unemployment, because of the direct influence unemployment has on government expenditures. Again GOVERNM is significant at the 5% level. In models inserting WORLD, however, GOVERNM no longer is significant (model 3).

Clear conclusions regarding the ideological influence on government spending cannot be drawn. If it is true that GOVERNM affects government spending, despite model 3 and despite the fact that MINISTER does not affect spending, there exists, to a certain extent, an ideological influence. This influence is not determined by the single fact whether or not the Social Democrats participate in government, but it is determined by some sort of ideological climate precipitated in ideological goals written down in government programmes.

Table 2.5   Total government spending (GOVSP)

	1	2	3
ARIMA	(1,1,4)	(1,1,3)	(1,1,2)
constant	0.77	0.64	1.37
	(3.16)	(2.62)	(3.52)
GOVERNM	3.32	3.24	1.00
	(2.25)	(2.31)	(0.43)
UR		0.05	
		(2.51)	
WORLD			-0.13
			(-3.22)
Q	5.34	5.80	7.80
(signif.)	(1.00)	(1.00)	(0.98)
DW	1.98	2.07	2.14
R^2	0.95	0.96	0.96

GOVSP: government spending (*rijksuitgaven*), nett in % nett national income (market prices), 1952-1992 (CPB)

The policy instruments are examined because the idea is that macroeconomic outcomes are difficult to manipulate. However, the same may be true for aggregated variables such as total government spending. It is also difficult to manipulate these variables, because government expenditures are often determined by long-term commitments. Therefore, it is not surprising that the exercises did not lead to a clear-cut conclusion.[22]

---

[22] Apart from total government spending, other aggregated variables were also examined. For the variables taxation (as a percentage of net national income), government deficit (as a percentage of net national income), and liquidity rate (M_2

Social Security Spending

Table 2.6   Social security spending (SOCSEC)

	1	2	3	4	5	6	7
ARIMA	(0,1,4)	(0,1,4)	(0,1,4)	(0,1,2)	(0,1,2)	(0,1,2)	(0,1,4)
constant	0.80	0.60	1.28	0.77	0.60	1.10	1.18
	(5.00)	(3.39)	(6.44)	(6.87)	(4.73)	(5.45)	(4.48)
AVERAGE	2.46			2.17			1.70
	(3.47)			(3.57)			(2.15)
MINISTER		1.21			1.04		
		(2.84)			(2.79)		
GOVERNM			4.38			3.31	
			(3.72)			(2.78)	
DUR				0.25	0.28	0.23	
				(2.97)	(3.14)	(2.67)	
WORLD							-0.11
							(-4.07)
Q	10.01	10.12		9.68	8.19	8.57	10.40
(signif.)	(0.93)	(0.93)		(0.94)	(0.98)	(0.97)	(0.92)
DW	1.98	1.96		1.95	1.96	2.00	1.92
R^2	0.99	0.99		0.99	0.99	0.99	1.00

SOCSEC: social security spending in % national income, 1952-1991 (CBS)

Finally, social security spending is examined. Van Dalen and Swank (1996, 1995a and b) concluded that the expenditures for social security (as well as for health care) increase during left-wing government terms. Right-wing governments, on the other hand, spend more on spending categories such as defense and infrastructure. This research demonstrated

---

divided by net national income) no significant ideological influences were found.

the existence of partisan cycles in the Netherlands. In this book only social security spending is examined.

In the first three models of table 2.6 all the coefficients of the ideology variables are significant at the 1% level. Even if the models (4, 5 and 6) take account of unemployment, the ideological influences remain statistically significant. In model 7 the variable WORLD is inserted. Now AVERAGE is significant at only the 5% level, whereas GOVERNM and MINISTER are no longer statistically significant (not reported; t-values of 1.53 and 1.44, respectively). Although this latter result somewhat tones down the conclusion, a positive correlation between social security spending and the ideological constitution of governments appears to be present. This result is comparable to the results of Van Dalen and Swank.

2.5 Conclusion

To start with, no empirical indications were found in favour of the partisan models with rational expectations. According to these models economic effects of left-wing policies are only transitory. No real effects in economic growth and employment were found in the first two years of left-wing governments.

The second conclusion is that there are indications of ideological influences on macroeconomic outcomes. However, these are not in accordance with the partisan theory. There is no additional economic growth, nor additional employment with left-wing governments. On the contrary, the models presented here demonstrated a negative correlation between the various ideology variables and the growth of national income and a positive correlation between these variables and unemployment. Inflation does rise with left-wing cabinets, as predicted by the partisan theory. This indicates that not only the political predictions did not come true, it also indicates that the economic assumption of the partisan theory is not satisfied, namely the assumption of a trade-off between inflation and unemployment - the Phillips curve. It seems as if there is no such trade-off in Dutch political economic interaction. Both unemployment and inflation increase with left-wing governments.

Influencing macroeconomic outcomes is a difficult matter, whereas it might be expected that economic policy variables may be easier to manipulate. This expectation came true only partially. Only for total government spending was an ideological effect found, but this did not lead to a clear-cut conclusion of ideological manipulation of this variable. No influences were found for other aggregated variables, such as the government deficit or taxation. A succesful strategy seems to be to investigate disaggregated spending categories. A partisan cycle was found for social security spending. This result is in accordance with the results of Van Dalen and Swank.

Finally, it is remarkable that the variable GOVERNM in the exercises with macroeconomic outcomes does not lead to satisfying results, but does lead to statistically significant results in the exercises with the policy variables. In the latter exercises the variables MINISTER and AVERAGE are not statistically significant. This difference may be explained by the fact that objectives regarding government spending are more clearly negotiated and described in government programmes than the macroeconomic goals unemployment and inflation.

The picture that seems to emerge from the empirical exercises is the following one: although the partisan models do not adequately describe political economic interaction in the Netherlands, there exists an ideological effect in the Dutch economy. It seems as if macroeconomic performance deteriorates with left-wing governments. At the same time government spending is raised, especially spending on social security. It is not possible to explain these results without a theory. Questions that need to be answered are: how did the oil crisis of the 1970s, which broke out just during one of the most left-wing government terms of the Netherlands, influence economic policies? What was the role of the labour movement and the employers' organizations? How does the institutional structure of a country influence economic policy? These kinds of questions are investigated in chapter four, just as the hypothesis that seems to emerge from the results of the present chapter: left-wing governments in the Netherlands are more interested in incomes policies (social security policies) than in policies to stimulate employment. Reference was already made to the research of Van Wijck. Without appropriate data (sufficiently long time series) an empirical examination of this hypothesis in the way of the present chapter is not possible. In chapter four a general framework is used to describe Dutch political economic interaction from 1973 until 1998. Before that, in chapter three the models of the political business cycle are subjected to an empirical investigation.

3 Electoral Politics in the Dutch Economy

3.1 Introduction

There is a large body of political and economic research on the factors playing a role in the electoral choices of voters. There is a measure of consensus about the idea that economic variables are important for the popularity of governments (see, for a survey of the literature, Nannestad and Paldam, 1994). Political business cycle models usually neglect voting behaviour and just assume that it is the economy that determines the electoral choices of voters: 'it's the economy, stupid!' This assumption leads to the observation that politicians wish the economy to look good around election time. Therefore, as was noted in chapter one, the timing of elections may well be affecting economic policies. It is a persuasive argument that governments would want to try to manipulate the economy to enhance electoral chances at the next general election.

However, the search for empirical evidence for political business cycle models has not been very succesful. The lack of evidence for the models from the 1970s has led to diminishing research efforts in the beginning of the 1980s. Later on in the 1980s a second wave of research was brought about by the incorporation of rational expectations in political economic models. Despite theoretical alterations the search for empirical evidence still did not lead to clear-cut results indicating that the political busines cycle argument really is an important argument with respect to formulating economic policies. Although the argument that politicians would like to manipulate the economy to enhance electoral chances remains persuasive, the pattern may not be as systematic as the models imply.

Nevertheless, in this chapter it is investigated whether the theory of the political business cycle has any empirical relevance for the Netherlands. There is not too much research on political economic cycles in this country. In general it is assumed that political business cycles do not exist in the Netherlands because of the fact that the government always consists of a coalition of political parties. In chapter one it was concluded that the methodological individualistic basis of the political business cycle theory, assuming that politicians are vote maximizers, has theoretical shortcomings if it is used to empirically test whether economic policies of governments are determined by electoral motives. The problems become even bigger if the government does not consist of only one political party, with a major role for the leader of the government, but of a coalition of parties. To assume that coalition governments are only interested in winning elections seems too simple an assumption. In addition, it seems inconceivable that political parties in a coalition government are able to pursue policies to enlarge their popularity.

Another complicating factor for the Dutch situation is the fact that government terms are not necessarily fixed periods of four years. Early elections may be called for if governments resign because of lack of support of the parliament. Remember, however, that the timing of elections is a deciding factor in the political business cycle theory.[1]

Van Dalen and Swank (1996, 1995a and b), already mentioned in the previous chapter, did provide evidence in favour of an electoral effect in the Dutch data, next to an ideological effect. They contested the results of Renaud and Van Winden (1987) who did not find evidence for political economic cycles in the Netherlands.[2] Van Dalen and Swank found evidence for electoral cycles in various spending variables: expenditures for defense, for infrastructure, for social security, for education and public administration. By examining spending variables they tested the models of the political business cycle with rational expectations of Rogoff and Sibert (1988) and Rogoff (1990). In these models vote maximizing politicians may increase government spending on 'highly visible projects' in election years to signal their competency to incompletely informed voters (Van Dalen and Swank, 1996). The results of Van Dalen and Swank are somewhat in contrast to the models of Rogoff and Sibert,

---

[1] The possibility of endogeneous elections is neglected in this book. In countries with endogeneous elections - the United Kingdom, for example - politicians may try to plan the next general election at an economically favourable point of time, instead of manipulating economic policies.

[2] Renaud and Van Winden (1987) tested the Frey and Schneider model for the Netherlands. As explained in chapter one, this model combines the partisan theory and the theory of the political business cycle.

because they found increased spending in election years on all the spending categories they examined and not just on the highly visible projects.

In this chapter it is examined whether electoral motives affect the Dutch economy. In section two macroeconomic data and in section three economic policy variables are subjected to empirical investigation. Thus, the structure of this chapter resembles the structure of the previous one. Moreover, the same data are used as well as the same empirical method. For the purpose of the empirical tests a number of political variables are used.

3.2 Macroeconomic Outcomes

In the Netherlands elections do not occur with perfect regularity as, for example, in the United States, where elections take place every four years in November. If the government has not enough support of the parliament, it may resign before the government's term of office is completed. In that case early elections - earlier than the planned election date - may be necessary. The timing of elections, however, plays an important role in the political business cycle theories, for it is the timing of elections that determines economic policy. To test the models of the political business cycle for the Dutch situation a number of binary electoral variables are constructed (see the list of symbols at the end of the book). The first variable - A - refers to all the election years in the Netherlands. All the other variables are variations of variable A. Variations are made in the precise timing of the election years; a distinction is made between elections after centre-left and centre-right government periods, as, for example, Lindbeck (1976) and Alesina, Cohen and Roubini (1993) suggested; and a distinction is made between planned elections after more or less completed government terms and early elections.[3] These are the variables that are used to test whether there is an electoral effect to be found in the Dutch data.

---

[3] Haynes and Stone (1989, 1990) also suggested to use electoral variables that describe the entire electoral period. Experiments with such variables for the Netherlands did not lead to satisfying results, possibly because the electoral periods vary too much in duration.

The first empirical analyses concern the macroeconomic data: the growth of national income and unemployment. These are the main variables in the traditional political business cycle models. If Dutch governments are opportunistic, as these models expect, they should be trying to stimulate economic growth and employment when the elections are imminent. In the next section the economic policy variables are examined.

Growth of Real National Income

To get some insight into the economic development and the timing of the elections, figure 3.1 depicts all Dutch election years and the growth figures of real national income. In table 3.1 the results of the empirical analyses are reported. Only the empirically significant results are presented in this table.

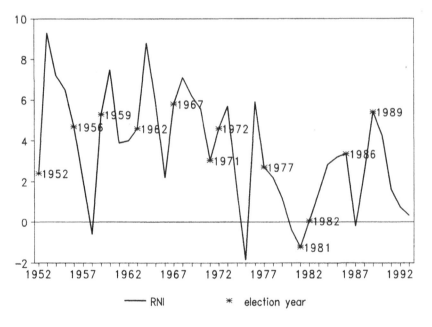

Figure 3.1 The growth of real national income and all election years

All electoral variables are tested with the help of ARIMA models. The models 1 and 2 are the only ones with statistically significant results for the electoral variables. The variable D_L - election years after more or less completed centre-left governments - is negatively correlated with the growth of national income and is significant at the 5% level. Inserting a constant does hardly change the results. However, variable D_L is based on a few data only: it takes the value one in 1956, 1977 and 1993. These are the election years after (almost) completed centre-left government terms.[4] Figure 3.1 indeed shows declining growth figures in these years. This result is in contrast to the expectation of political business cycle theory.

For the electoral variables in the models that take account of the international economic developments - the variable WORLD (growth of world trade) - there are more significant results. Each time an ARIMA(2,1,2) model was used, sometimes with, sometimes without a constant. Models 3 and 4 show, strangely enough, opposite results. Model 3 used variable A - all elections - whereas model 4 used variable D - only the planned elections.

In the models 5, 6 and 7 the variables that distinguish between elections after centre-left and centre-right governments are examined. The picture gets somewhat clearer. Here only the statistically significant results are reported, but for the other variables the same is true: there are negative signs for the variables referring to the elections after centre-left government periods and positive signs for the variables referring to the elections after centre-right government terms. In models 5 and 7 the coefficients for the variables D_L and B_L have a negative sign and are statistically significant at at least the 5% level. Although not significant (and therefore not reported), the other variable referring to elections after centre-left governments, variable A_L, has also a negative sign. By contrast, variable A_R in model 6 has a positive sign, as have the variables B_R and D_R (not significant, not reported). These variables refer to elections after centre-right government periods.

It is not possible to draw clear-cut conclusions from these exercises. There are relatively few statistically significant results and some results are even contradictory. However, it is remarkable that the variables distinguishing between elections after centre-left and centre-right government periods have opposite signs. These results seem to support the results of the previous chapter (partisan theory), rather than to suggest

---

[4] Because the elections were early in 1994, 1993 is arbitrarily chosen as the election year for cabinet Lubbers/Kok.

that centre-left and centre-right governments use different electoral strategies.

Table 3.1   Real national income (RNI)

	1	2	3	4	5	6	7
ARIMA	(0,1,4)	(0,1,4)	(2,1,2)	(2,1,2)	(2,1,2)	(2,1,2)	(2,1,2)
constant		0.14	-0.62			-0.42	
		(0.77)	(-2.52)			(-2.59)	
A			1.80				
			(2.44)				
A_R						1.50	
						(2.52)	
B_L							-1.19
							(-3.12)
D				-0.87			
				(-2.13)			
D_L	-3.10	-3.45			-2.36		
	(-2.82)	(-2.86)			(-3.92)		
DWORLD			0.37	0.28	0.27	0.36	0.33
			(6.19)	(6.11)	(5.69)	(7.24)	(5.74)
Q	8.47	8.94	7.37	10.13	9.82	9.13	7.00
(signif.)	(0.97)	(0.96)	(0.99)	(0.93)	(0.94)	(0.96)	(0.99)
DW	1.75	1.77	1.68	1.92	2.11	1.77	1.90
R^2	0.33	0.34	0.78	0.76	0.77	0.79	0.75

A: all election years
A_R: all election years after centre-right government periods
B_L: years of and one year before elections after centre-left government periods
D: election years after more or less completed government periods
D_L: election years after more or less completed centre-left government periods

Unemployment

Figure 3.2 shows the growth of employment in the market sector along with all election years in the Netherlands. In seven of the eleven election years there is no growth of employment; most of the times there is even a decline of employment in the market sector. This figure shows no signs of pre-electoral stimulation of the Dutch economy. For the econometric analyses two data sources are used: CPB data for Dutch unemployment (UR) and the change in volume of employment in the market sector (EMPL), and OECD data for Dutch and European unemployment figures (URNL and UREC).

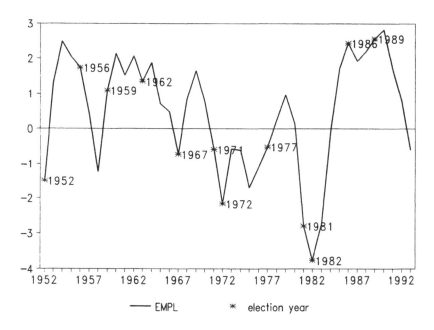

Figure 3.2 Volume change of employment in the market sector and all election years

ARIMA(4,1,0) models satisfy the statistical requirements for the estimation of the unemployment (UR) models. Inserting a constant does not drastically change the results. Model 1 in table 3.2 is an example of these models. None of the electoral variables have statistically significant coefficients.

Table 3.2   Unemployment and employment in the market sector

	1 UR	2 UR	3 URNL	4 EMPL	5 EMPL
ARIMA	(4,1,0)	(4,1,0)	(6,1,0)	(1,1,2)	(1,1,2)
constant		1.00	-0.19	0.13	0.18
		(2.53)	(-1.17)	(0.85)	(1.59)
A	0.53		0.59	-0.61	
	(1.67)		(2.58)	(-1.48)	
A_R					-1.25
					(-3.48)
C_A		0.74			
		(2.03)			
DUREC			0.91		
			(4.49)		
WORLD		-0.14			
		(-3.52)			
Q	5.87	6.83	7.53	5.72	7.13
(signif.)	(1.00)	(0.99)	(0.94)	(1.00)	(0.99)
DW	2.05	2.15	2.01	1.81	1.78
R^2	0.95	0.96	0.98	0.57	0.74

A: all election years
A_R: all election years after centre-right government periods
C_A: one year after election years after more or less completed government periods

Model 2 in this table takes account of the international economic circumstances by inserting WORLD as a variable. Model 2, with C_A as the electoral variable, is the only model with a statistically significant electoral variable (positive correlation). For models using the OECD data few ARIMA models were found that satisfy the statistical conditions: the values for Q were too low and the coefficients were unreliable. Only for variable A a suitable model was found: ARIMA(6,1,0), with or without a constant (model 3). The variable is significant at the 2% level (positive correlation). However, the results for the other variables cast doubts on the reliability and robustness of this model.

Models 4 and 5 show the results of some of the exercises with the time series EMPL (volume change of employment in the market sector). For each electoral variable a ARIMA(1,1,2) model was suitable. Only variable A_R has a statistically significant coefficient, a negative one. Variable A is not significant, but has a negative sign as well. In conclusion, there are no indications for a traditional political business cycle in the Netherlands. There is no pre-electoral stimulation of the Dutch economy. On the contrary, the results point to decreasing employment in election years, while unemployment increases. There is no additional employment in election years to satisfy myopic voters.

3.3 Economic Policy

For the traditional political business cycle theory the results of the previous section are disappointing. In the present section economic policy variables are tested empirically. There are various reasons for examining economic policy instruments rather than macroeconomic outcomes. One reason is that it may be that governments would like to manipulate macroeconomic outcomes, but that they do not know whether they will succeed. By examining the policy instruments it can be established whether governments tried to influence the economy for electoral purposes. Additionally, as some theories assume, it is not only easier for governments to manipulate policy instruments, but it is also more clearly visible to voters. Tufte (1978) focused on government spending and social security transfers ('mail them larger checks'), because he believed that these instruments have a more direct influence on disposable income of voters, than employment policies. The models of Rogoff and Sibert (1988) and Rogoff (1990) focus on taxation policy, government spending and money growth. These models, taking account of the rational expectations hypothesis, assume that political budget cycles are realized because of temporary information asymmetries between voters and the government. Voters do not exactly know the competence of the incumbent politicians. The politicians use clearly visible policy instruments to signal their competence to voters, knowing, however, that there are no significant or lasting economic effects to be expected from their policies.

The variables examined in this section are: the government deficit, total government spending and social security spending. The latter two were also examined in the previous chapter.[5] Note that these variables are defined as a percentage of national income. It is therefore possible that the results for the political variables are caused by the denominator, that is, by changes in national income. This effect is neglected in the present analysis. It was also neglected in the previous chapter. By examining these kinds of variables, it is assumed that governments directly adjust policies to changes in national income.

Government Deficit

Figure 3.3 (GOVDEF(t)-GOVDEF(t-1)) shows that in seven of the eleven election years the government deficit is decreasing, instead of increasing as the political business cycle theory predicts. In general, the peaks of increasing government deficits seem to take place somewhere in the middle of the government's term of office, not at the end. In election years the government deficit decreases, or increases at a smaller rate than in previous years. Only in 1981 and 1971 the government deficit increased more than it did in the previous year. It seems as if Dutch governments do not use increasing deficits to finance a larger popularity at the elections. However, it is remarkable that the governments that pursue austerity goals and try to lower the deficit - the centre-right governments in the periods 1967-1971, 1982-1986 and 1986-1989 - do so at a lower rate in election years.

For testing the correlation of the electoral variables with the government deficit ARMA(2,0) models were used (table 3.3). In model 1 the coefficient for variable A is not significant; for variable D in model 2 it is significant at only the 10% level, whereas the significance level for variable A_L in model 4 lies around 10%. Only variable D_L in model 3 is clearly statistically significant at the 2% level.

---

[5] Other variables examined are taxation (as a percentage of net national income) and the liquidity rate (M_2 divided by net national income). These examinations were not successful. No electoral effect was found in these data. For monetary instruments this is not surprising, according to Van Dalen and Swank (1995b: 2): 'the Netherlands has almost always participated in a fixed exchange rate regime'.

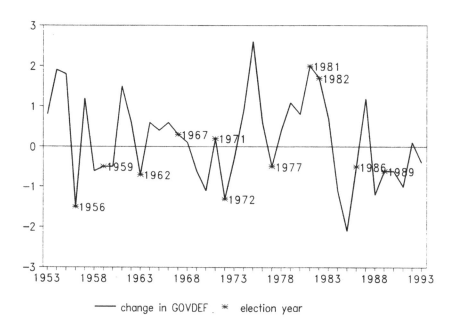

Figure 3.3 Change in the government deficit and all election years

All the coefficients of the electoral variables have negative signs, including the ones not reported. The econometric results, however, do not allow clear-cut conclusions. There is no indication of Dutch governments manipulating the deficit in order to enhance electoral chances. On the contrary, it seems as if governments want to demonstrate frugality in election years. Is frugality what Dutch voters want to see from their governments, whereas, for example, American voters want their governments to spend more? This question is beyond the scope of this book.[6]

---

[6] In a survey article on the political economy of budget deficits Alesina and Perotti (1995) state that the political business cycle models are not well equipped to explain long term trends in government deficits. Models that take account of the party structure are more successful (for example, the larger the number of parties in a coalition, the higher the deficit).

Table 3.3   Government deficit (GOVDEF)

	1	2	3	4
ARIMA	(2,0,0)	(2,0,0)	(2,0,0)	(2,0,0)
constant	4.21	4.29	4.32	4.12
	(2.71)	(2.68)	(2.73)	(2.74)
A	-0.28			
	(-1.30)			
A_L				-0.60
				(-1.70)
D		-0.44		
		(-1.78)		
D_L			-0.94	
			(-2.47)	
Q	9.02	8.60	10.80	8.78
(signif.)	(0.96)	(0.97)	(0.90)	(0.96)
DW	1.91	1.94	1.87	1.85
R^2	0.89	0.89	0.90	0.89

A: all election years
A_L: all election years after centre-left government periods
D: election years after more or less completed government periods
D_L: election years after more or less completed centre-left government periods

Total Government Spending

According to public opinion spending more money during election years is probably the most likely electoral strategy, irrespective of the fact whether more spending takes place as part of Keynesian employment policies or just to do 'nice things' for the voters. Figure 3.4 portrays the change in total government spending as a percentage of net national income (GOVSP(t)-GOVSP(t-1)) and all Dutch election years. This figure shows no signs of pre-electoral extra spending. The peaks in this figure, indicating increasing government spending, are most of the time situated somewhere in the middle of government periods. It is remarkable that in election years spending often decreases.

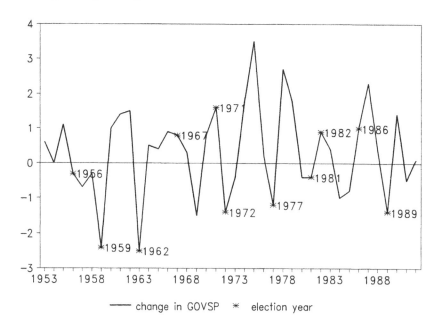

Figure 3.4 Change in total government spending and all election years

Table 3.4 presents the results of the empirical analyses. For most of the models ARIMA(0,1,4) seems to be the appropriate specification. For some models a different specification was necessary. For model 1, with electoral variable A, ARIMA(0,1,9) seems suitable. The coefficient for the electoral variable is highly significant and negatively correlated with government spending. Except for the variables C_B and C_A - one year before and one year after election years - all coefficients of the electoral variables that do not discriminate between centre-left or centre-right governments have negative signs, but are not significant. Variable C_A has a positive sign, but is also not significant; C_B has a positive sign and is significant at only the 10% level (model 2).

The variables that do discriminate between the two types of governments also have negative signs, except for variable B_L, but this variable has no statistically significant coefficient. The models 3 to 5 present statistically significant results: A_L has a significant coefficient at the 5% level, A_R at 10% and D_L at 2%.[7]

Table 3.4   Total government spending (GOVSP)

	1	2	3	4	5
ARIMA	(0,1,9)	(0,1,7)	(0,1,4)	(0,1,6)	(0,1,4)
constant	0.84	0.14	0.42	0.58	0.41
	(4.80)	(1.00)	(1.62)	(3.18)	(1.86)
A	-1.58				
	(-5.62)				
A_L			-1.24		
			(-2.28		
A_R				-0.95	
				(-1.90)	
C_B		1.14			
		(1.83)			
D_L					-1.52
					(-2.54)
Q	9.84	9.41	8.56	7.32	8.14
(signif.)	(0.94)	(0.95)	(0.97)	(0.99)	(0.98)
DW	1.94	1.95	2.05	2.03	2.07
R^2	0.97	0.95	0.95	0.97	0.95

A: all election years
A_L: all election years after centre-left government periods
A_R: all election years after centre-right government periods
C_B: year before election years after more or less completed government periods
D_L: election years after more or less completed centre-left government periods

---

[7] Attempts were made to incorporate WORLD or UR in the models to take account explicitly of international or unemployment influences on spending. No significant or reliable coefficients were found for these variables.

In sum, there are no signs of a political business cycle in government spending. In other words, Dutch governments do not seem to try to buy popularity during election years. On the contrary, it seems as if spending decreases in election years. This result is in accordance with the results of the analyses of the government deficit.

Social Security Spending

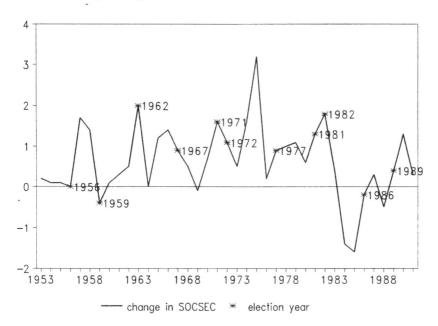

Figure 3.5 Change in social security spending and all election years

The last policy variable examined in this chapter is the variable SOCSEC: total social security spending. It is one of the variables that was examined by Van Dalen and Swank (1995a and b). They found an electoral effect in social security expenditures. Their method as well as their data differ from the method and data used in this book.[8] Figure 3.5 (SOCSEC(t)-SOCSEC(t-1)) gives no indication of the existence of a political business cycle in social security spending. However, it is remarkable that in 1962,

---

[8] Van Dalen and Swank used a structural model of government spending to test for political effects on various categories of public spending.

1971, 1977 and 1981 the rise in social security spending is higher than in the preceding year, whereas in 1986 and 1989 - with the 1980s as a period of austerity measures - the decline in social security spending is smaller than in the preceding year. In fact, in 1989 social security spending increased again.

Table 3.5   Social security spending (SOCSEC)

	1	2	3
ARIMA	(0,1,4)	(0,1,2)	(0,1,4)
constant	0.48	0.58	0.72
	(2.09)	(3.20)	(3.83)
A	0.51	0.10	
	(1.81)	(0.35)	
C_B			-0.65
			(-2.23)
DUR		0.34	0.31
		(3.19)	(2.92)
Q	10.78	9.16	9.41
(signif.)	(0.90)	(0.96)	(0.95)
DW	1.99	1.98	1.98
R^2	0.99	0.99	0.99

A: all election years
C_B: year before election years after more or less completed government periods

Nevertheless, the econometric analyses, reported in table 3.5, do not provide evidence for electoral strategies regarding social security spending. For most of the electoral variables ARIMA(0,1,4) models were used; for a few ARIMA(0,1,2). Only variable A has a significant coefficient (at the 10% level) and is positively correlated with social security spending (model 1). All other variables were not significant, and there was no pattern discovered in the signs of the coefficients. In models 2 and 3 the change in unemployment is inserted as a variable to explicitly take account of the effect of unemployment on social security spending. In this exercise the coefficient of variable A is no longer significant (model 2). Variable C_B - year before election years - is the only variable with a statistically significant coefficient. It is negatively correlated with social security spending.

To conclude, there are no clear signs of a political business cycle in social security spending. However, figure 3.5 and the exercises seem to hint at some sort of electoral influence. It seems as if the significant rises in spending occur before the election years, whereas the significant decreases in social security spending also seem to happen before the election years. Especially the latter observation may be pointing at an electoral strategy. It may also simply indicate that government goals were already reached before election years. Anyhow, in contrast to the research of Van Dalen and Swank no obvious additional social security spending in election years was found. Their method was successful in finding political business cycles in various categories of public spending, including social security spending.

3.4 Conclusion

In the Netherlands elections do not take place with perfect regularity. This questions the relevance of political business cycle theory for the Dutch situation in advance. Nevertheless, to test the theory anyway, it means that a number of electoral variables have to be used to take account of the varying timing of elections. In the present chapter the exercises with twelve different variables were reported. Variations were made in the precise timing of elections; a distinction was made between early elections and planned elections and a distinction was made between elections after centre-left and centre-right governments.

With so many different variables, it is not surprising that some variables have significant coefficients. Many of the variables are based on a few data only. The significance of one coefficient may therefore just be a matter of coincidence. On average there were not too many significant results. Some variables that had significant coefficients had a sign opposite to the theoretically expected one. There is no political business cycle in the macroeconomic variables growth and unemployment. On the contrary, the results for the variable growth of national income seem to support the results of the previous chapter: there were indications of partisan differences. The outcomes for unemployment were contradictory to political business cycle theory: increasing unemployment in election years. In short, there is no traditional - Nordhaus - political business cycle in the Netherlands.

There were more significant results for the economic policy variables. But, again, the results contradicted the expectations of the theory. The government deficit does not increase and there is no extra government spending in election years. Yet, there are small signs of electoral influences, be it that they are opposite to theoretical expectations. The coefficients conspicuously often have negative signs, and sometimes are indeed significant. Considering these results and looking at the figures it seems as if policy goals are pursued in the beginning or in the middle of a government's term of office, but not at the end. The significant increases or decreases of government spending occurred before the last year of a government's term of office. In election years there seems to be a tendency of frugality in government policies. This could point to governments wanting to be elected in order to choose policies, instead of governments choosing policies in order to win elections.[9] Anyhow, there is no traditional political business cycle in the Netherlands. Although there seems to be some influence of the timing of elections, Dutch politicians do not try to buy popularity in election years. Pursuing policies seems to be more important than winning elections.

This concludes the empirical investigation of the political economic interaction models. Although an ideological effect was found in the Dutch data, the partisan model, tested empirically in chapter three, does not adequately describe politics in the Dutch economy. Even less empirical support was found for the political business cycle. This model is also too simple and too mechanistic to describe political economic interaction in the Netherlands. In the next chapter a general framework is used to describe politics and economics in the Netherlands. This framework incorporates the interaction of governments with the labour movement and employers' organizations. In addition, attention is paid to the electoral consequences of chosen strategies and policies.

---

[9] 'In a Downsian model (where parties care only about winning), the parties choose policy in order to win elections, whereas in a partisan model the parties want to be elected in order to choose policies' (Alesina and Rosenthal, 1995: 17).

4 Institutional Interaction in the Netherlands

4.1 Introduction

In chapter one it was concluded that the political business cycle models and the models of the partisan theory are too mechanistic and that they do not take account of institutional factors that influence the policy choices of governments. However, comparative political economics, which does take account of other institutional actors than governments only, was also criticized. It was criticized mainly for being too structuralistic. Finally, the model of Scharpf (1987, 1991) was described. This model emphasizes the economic and political circumstances affecting the interaction between political actors, and analyses why certain policy choices are made. Scharpf defines two games: an electoral game in which governments have to take account of the electoral consequences of their policies and a coordination game between the government and the labour movement determining the success of government policy. The model was described in chapter one.

In the second section of this chapter a framework is developed - akin to Scharpf's model - that is used to analyse political economic interaction in the Netherlands. Ideological partisan goals and electoral strategies are two factors playing a role in this framework. The objective of this chapter is to demonstrate that this analytical framework presents a more complete explanation of partisan goals and electoral motives regarding Dutch economic policy than the models of the political business cycle and the partisan theory. Additionally, it is shown that the institutionalized labour movement and the employers' organizations play an important role in the Netherlands - the Dutch model. These two political actors are ignored by the abstract models of the political business cycle and the partisan theory. Even Scharpf did not take account of the employers' organizations.

Section three consists of a brief survey of the main characteristics (and the historical development) of the Dutch political economic institutions. The players are introduced and the (development of the) rules of the game are explained. In section four political economic interaction is analysed for the period 1973-1998 using the analytical framework developed in section two. The purpose of this chapter is to demonstrate that ideology matters in the Dutch economy, as was concluded in chapter three. Unlike chapter three, this chapter describes how, why and when it mattered.

4.2 A Simple Analytical Framework

Scharpf's model was dealt with in chapter one. This model, which pays much attention to the strategic policy choices of the political actors, inspired the design of the following framework, although there are significant differences. For example, Scharpf's model was constructed to compare the various policy choices of four countries (Austria, Great Britain, Sweden and West Germany) in especially the 1970s and early 1980s, whereas the intention of the present chapter is limited to the description of the policy choices of the polical actors in the Netherlands between 1973 and 1998. By explaining Dutch political economic interaction the differences with Scharpf's model become visible.

In the Dutch situation the following political actors are of importance. First there is the government, consisting of various political parties. The Christian Democrats (CDA) almost always take part, whereas the Social Democrats (PvdA) and the Conservative Liberals (VVD) alternate in government. Thus, the latter two parties make the government respectively a centre-left or a centre-right government.[1] The ideological goals of cabinets are a compromise between the goals of the constituting parties. The goals of the parties are assumed to be determined by the interests of their core constituencies. Scharpf considered three voter groups: lower, middle and upper income groups. In the present framework these groups are assumed to be the core constituencies of the three most important political parties. The lower income groups are considered to be the core constituency of the Social Democrats (and other left-wing parties); the upper income groups are considered to be the core

---

[1] Sometimes smaller political parties take part in the government as well. D66 (Social Liberals) and the PPR (Left-wing Radicals) participated in Cabinet Den Uyl (1973-1977). D66 also took part in the Cabinets Van Agt II and III (1981-1982) and Cabinet Kok (1994-1998).

constituency of the Conservative Liberal party; and the middle income groups the core constituency of all three political movements, but the Christian Democrats in particular.

The lower income groups prefer government policies aimed at redistribution of income in general and employment and social security policies in particular. The upper income groups especially benefit from low inflation and low taxation policies. The preferences of the middle income groups depend on the economic circumstances and vary from lower taxation to more social security spending. In this division of the voter groups the usual notions of the preferences of voters of left-wing and right-wing political parties are followed (see, for example, Hibbs, 1987a). In Scharpf's model there is a pivotal role to be played by the middle group of voters alternating its voting behaviour for the two possible governments depending on economic circumstances. In the present framework this pivotal role may be regarded to be played by the Christian Democrats and their voters.[2]

The second political actor is the labour movement. The organization of the labour movement in the Netherlands is explained in the next section. Although it is perhaps an extreme simplification to consider the labour movement as one political actor, it is useful to make this simplifying assumption at this stage. Wages, employment and social security are considered to be the main objectives of the members of the labour unions.

The third political actor consists of the cooperation of employers' organizations. The specific role of the employers' organizations in the Netherlands is also explained in the next section. It really is a simplifying assumption to consider these organizations as one political actor. According to Scharpf employers' organizations - *capital* - do not decide on macroeconomic policy. They cannot be considered to be one political actor. Wilke (1991a) is of the same opinion by stating that investments are not an issue of bargaining. However, it is shown in the next section that at the national level employers' organizations do play an important role in the Netherlands. It may be that the central employers' organizations cannot (or will not) use investments as an issue of bargaining, but there is always the threat of less private investments or a

---

[2] Note, however, that in the Netherlands election outcomes are not always decisive with regard to the formation of coalition cabinets (see, for example, De Swaan, 1982 and Therborn, 1989).

flight of capital abroad causing more unemployment. Moreover, these organizations are part of the institutional organization of Dutch labour relations and therefore influence the way in which decisions on macroeconomic policy are made. Their main objectives are low wages, inflation and taxation - in other words, low production costs.

Central in Scharpf's analysis is the contrast between Keynesian and monetarist macroeconomic policy and the consequences for inflation and unemployment. Whether left-wing governments do follow their preferred Keynesian policies and right-wing governments monetarist policies, is dependent on economic circumstances - oil crisis inflation and wage policy by the labour unions, whose actions are determined by short-term economic self-interest - and the electoral consequences of various policies (with a decisive role for the middle group of voters). In the analysis in this chapter the emphasis is not only on the difference between these two general lines of policy, although they play their role, but on the specific policy goals of the various political actors as well. Especially social security policies (and incomes policy in general) are important in Dutch political economic interaction.

The working mechanism of Scharpf's model is determined by the assumption that labour unions only act on the basis of economic self-interest. If the government follows a Keynesian policy, labour unions may follow an agressive wage policy without running the risk of higher unemployment.[3] In contrast, if the government follows a monetarist policy, the labour movement may be more careful with its wage demands to protect existing employment. Subject to these policy reactions of the labour unions, partisan governments choose their electoral strategy. In his model Scharpf explained that left-wing governments in various countries at the end of the 1970s switched from Keynesian to monetarist policies (see also Hood, 1994). He compared the different policy reactions of the governments to the international economic crisis in the 1970s. For this purpose, and to provide more exact hypotheses about the strategic policy choices of governments, Scharpf's model was more precisely formulated than the framework in the present chapter. The framework used in the present chapter has an illustrative character, which is the reason that it has no strictly defined working mechanism. The framework is only used as an

---

[3] Scharpf does not take account of the possibility of lower economic growth in the future. Lower economic growth may result in smaller wage gains in the future (Kenworthy, 1990).

instrument to describe Dutch political economic interaction and to comment on the empirical findings of chapters two and three.

There are two games governments can play: they can turn left or they can turn right (*linksom* or *rechtsom*). The natural way for centre-left governments is to turn left. By trading off social security and Keynesian demand management policies for wage moderation by the labour movement the well-known advantageous corporatist interaction game is played. Whether the economic outcomes really are advantageous is subject to international economic influences and to the extent the labour movement really succeeds in moderating wage claims while the government concentrates on employment policies.

Centre-right governments are assumed to prefer to turn right. Their priorities are low inflation and low taxation. They hope to stimulate investments and employment in the private sector by aiming at lower production costs for the supply side of the economy. They consider the employers' organizations as their natural allies.

These two 'games' resemble the two best possible worlds of the theories of, for example, Calmfors and Driffill (1988) and Lange and Garrett (1985) and Garrett and Lange (1986). These theories were meant to compare the macroeconomic outcomes of these different games of institutional interaction. The intention here is not to show which game or which instititutional context performs best, but to analyse why certain policy choices were made in the Netherlands.

Scharpf emphasized the importance of the strategic policy choices of the political actors - notably governments - in distinct situations. Traxler (1990) suggests, additionally, a theory of political exchange between capital and labour to analyse corporatist interaction between these two actors. In his view exchange relations determine the form (varying over time and from country to country) of what he calls interest governance - that is to what extent the interests of interest groups are represented by government policies. The intention of the present framework is to discuss the exchange relations between all the political actors, namely between the government and the labour movement, between the government and the employers' organizations and also between the labour movement and the employers' organizations. The two government games go together with the interaction between the labour movement and employers' organizations. The employers' organizations and the labour movement try to exchange employment for wage moderation.

This framework is used in section four to describe the policy choices of the Dutch governments in the period 1973-1998. But first the main characteristics of the Dutch political economic institutions are described, as well as the most important economic developments since 1945. Moreover, it is necessary to get somewhat better acquainted with the leading players of the Dutch political game. This is done in the following section.

4.3 Main Characteristics of Dutch Institutions and Political Actors

The institutional structure determining the way in which macroeconomic policies are decided upon is not an unchanging reality. Such a structure evolves over time, depending on economic and political circumstances. The development of the institutional structure goes together with changes of the political actors. New actors come into play, old actors disappear. It is not the purpose of this section to give a precise account of the evolving institutional structure since 1945. However, it is necessary to sketch the main lines of development since that point in time.

The story of reconstruction of the Dutch economy after World War II has been told by many authors. Well-known are, for example, the textbooks of Windmuller, De Galan and Van Zweeden (1983), Reynaerts and Nagelkerke (1986) and Albeda and Dercksen (1994). The studies of Hemerijck (1992) and Van Kersbergen (1995) discussed, respectively, the historical development of Dutch corporatism and the specific role of Christian Democratic thought in the development of the welfare state. All these authors extensively described how during the first 25 years after the war the Dutch welfare state characteristics and the corporatist institutions of policy-making took shape.[4] Here is a brief summary of the most important developments.

Economic reconstruction after the war was a national effort. Especially wage and incomes policy formed an important policy field for the national political actors. These policies were centrally coordinated at the national level. It all started with the Extraordinary Decree on Industrial Relations of 1945 (*Buitengewoon Besluit Arbeidsverhoudingen*).

---

[4] For an account stressing the political aspects of Dutch policy-making, see Gladdish (1991). Fortuyn (1983) discussed the economic developments of the Netherlands since 1945.

The Board of Government Mediators (*College van Rijksbemiddelaars*), the Foundation of Labour (*Stichting van de Arbeid*), and the Social and Economic Council (*Sociaal Economische Raad, SER*) were the main - corporatist - institutions that came into existence in the post war years. The Board of Government Mediators and the Foundation of Labour were established in 1945 as a result of the Extraordinary Decree on Industrial Relations. The SER was established in 1950.

Until the end of the 1950s the governments had been dominated by a coalition between the Social Democratic and confessional political parties, especially the Catholic party (KVP). It was this coalition of political movements that determined the construction of corporatist institutions after the war. There was consensus about the idea that the representatives of the labour movement and the empoyers' organizations had to be incorporated in the sphere of public-policy-making. To rebuild the economy the government - in consultation with the formal institutions - had a determinative role with respect to wage and price developments. Under the direction of the minister of Social Affairs the Board of Mediators had the competence to set binding rules to control wages. The Board had the authority to accept or reject collective agreements (*CAOs*) or to declare them binding for a branch of industry. In other words, the Board to a large degree determined the wage developments. Before deciding, however, the Board had to consult the Foundation of Labour. This bipartite institution consists of the representatives of the labour movement and the employers' organizations. The Board of Mediators, and the government as a whole, consulted the Foundation about national economic issues. In this way the directive wage policies of the government were realized in consultation with the social partners.

In 1950 the SER was established. As Hemerijck (1992) and Van Kersbergen (1995) described, the establishment of the SER was the conclusion of an ideological debate between the various social and political movements about the institutional organization of the Dutch economy. In the words of Van Kersbergen (1995: 130) the SER was the result of 'conflicts between social democratic central planning conceptions and Catholic corporatist proposals'. As a part of the Industrial Organization Act of 1950 (*Wet op de Bedrijfsorganisatie*) the SER was established as an advisory body of the government on social and macroeconomic policies. It is a tripartite institution consisting of 15 representatives of the labour movement, 15 representatives of the employers and 15 independent members appointed by the government. By taking over some tasks of the Foundation of Labour it became more important than the Foundation. However, the Foundation was not abolished. It is still an institution in which bipartite collective bargaining takes place, especially on matters of working conditions (Hemerijck, 1992).

There was a high degree of consensus about the centralized institutional structure of Dutch industrial relations. It was an elite group of people that had control over macroeconomic and social policies. Centralization was a result of the post war coalition of the Social Democrats and the confessional parties as well as of the 'pillarized' social relations in Dutch society (Hemerijck, 1994a; Visser, 1992). Four pillars, the Catholics, the Protestants, the Socialists and the Liberals, had and still have their own political parties, labour unions, sports clubs, broadcasting organizations, and so forth. The leaders of the pillars, which are hierarchically organized, decide on political matters. As noted, incomes policies - and the construction of the Dutch social security system - were probably the most important policies for the political actors.

Both the labour movement and the employers' organizations are organized according to the pillarized system. This means that there are confessional labour unions and confessional employers' organizations next to socialist ones. Many of these organizations were gathered in a few central federations. The socialist unions were united in the NVV (Dutch Federation for Labour Unions), the confessional unions in the CNV (National Christian Federation) and in the NKV (Dutch Catholic Federation).[5] The NKV and the NVV merged into the FNV (Dutch Labour Federation) in 1976. The employers and their organizations are also united in a few central organizations. Apart from organizations for small and medium-sized businesses and agricultural organizations the two major ones are the VNO (Federation of Dutch Enterprises) and the NCW (Christian Employers' Federation). In 1968 business and employers' organizations merged into the VNO. In 1970 the NCW originated from the Catholic and Protestant federations. Both federations have connections with political parties; the NCW with the Christian Democrats, the VNO with both the Conservative Liberals and the Christian Democrats. In the early Seventies these federations became professional organizations with an increasing number of staff members and in 1974 the VNO appointed a

---

[5] The name of the Catholic federation was changed regularly. The name NKV is from 1963 (Reynaerts and Nagelkerke, 1986).

full time president (Albeda and Dercksen, 1994; Reynaerts and Nagelkerke, 1986; Visser, 1992).

This description of the labour movement and the employers' organizations shows that the institutional structure of a country is not a fixed reality. The Dutch corporatist institutions were established between 1945 and 1950, the period of reconstruction of the Dutch economy. From 1950 until around 1964, a period of strong economic growth, these institutions determined to a large extent the social economic policies in the Netherlands. However, the prosperous economic development of the 1950s and 1960s, causing tensions in the system, resulted in institutional changes. For example, the organizational changes in the labour movement and employers' organizations at the end of the 1960s and the beginning of the 1970s were caused by the polarization of the labour relations. As a result of the tight labour market - economic growth resulted in near full employment - the directive wage policies of the government became less effective in the 1960s. Employers and labour unions were given more freedom to bargain for higher wages. In 1963, 1964 and 1965 this led to 'wage explosions' of respectively 9%, 15% and 10.7 % (Windmuller, De Galan and Van Zweeden, 1983). Accompanied by intense discussions and confrontations with the labour movement, the government in 1970 replaced the Extraordinary Decree on Industrial Relations with the new Wage Act. The intention was to replace the directive wage policies with free wage bargaining. However, against the will of the labour movement, the government retained the possibility of intervening if wage demands were to high according to the government. Despite institutional changes, wage policy remained a matter of centralized discussions between the political actors.

Political scientists distinguish two phases in Dutch political economic relations. The first period, from 1945 until the mid-1960s, is the period of pillarization and consensus between the leaders of the pillars. The period following the mid-1960s is the period of depillarization and more adverse relations (Lijphart, 1989). Lijphart, commenting on his own research of the 1960s and on the research of Daalder in the 1970s, stressed that the differences between these periods must not be exaggerated. For example, many pillarized institutions still exist (see also Michels, 1993). Nevertheless, as Wolinetz (1990b: 405), among others, noted, since the mid-1960s 'politics has become a much more public process and political leaders must now go to greater efforts to mobilize consent'. Before the mid-1960s the pillarized political system - based on religious and class differences - was very stable. There were no huge electoral shifts, because voters were loyal to their political leaders. However, societal changes - religion and class factors becoming less important for voters - resulted in a more open political struggle (Irwin and Holsteyn, 1989). Before the mid-1960s 'there was ... a strong incentive towards an accommodationist style in politics ... reinforced by the commonly felt need to overcome the problems of post-war reconstruction and the decolonisation of the Dutch East Indies' (Tromp, 1989: 84). After 1965 depillarization and secularization led to an electoral decline for the confessional parties (KVP (Catholic party), ARP and CHU (two Protestant parties)), but also for the PvdA. New parties, of which D66 (Social Liberals) still prominently exists, emerged. New parties, dissident factions - the New Left in the PvdA, for example - and changes in voter preferences led to a polarization between the political parties (Tromp, 1989; Wolinetz, 1989).

Depillarization and polarized political relations between the political parties at the end of the 1960s ultimately led to the realization of the government presided by the Social Democratic Prime Minister Joop den Uyl. In the 1972 elections the PvdA won four extra seats in parliament, whereas the Catholics (KVP) lost seven. The confessional parties and the Liberals (VVD) lost their majority in parliament. The left-wing parties - PvdA, D66 and the PPR - claiming to have won the elections, demanded to constitute a cabinet based on their joint political programme which was called 'Turning point' (*Keerpunt*) (Wolinetz, 1989). The cabinet was dominated by left-wing ministers: seven for the PvdA, two for the PPR and one for D66. For the KVP there were four ministers and two for the ARP (Anti Revolutionary Party). In parliament the three left-wing parties had only 56 of the total of 150 seats, implying that although the cabinet may have been dominated by left-wing ministers, it needed the support of the confessional parties in parliament. The central slogan of this cabinet was the dispersion of knowledge, income and power. In addition, the cabinet stressed the importance of well-being policy next to policies to stimulate and redistribute material prosperity. Other radical plans were related to land policy, capital growth redistribution, democracy in the firm and a new investment policy (Lehning, 1989: 180).[6]

---

[6] These radical proposals, however, were never carried out; the government simply lacked the support of the confessional parties in parliament for these proposals (Lehning, 1989).

Due to the liberalization of wage policies, with an intended smaller role for the government, and due to the economic situation with unemployment relatively low (but rising) the political position of the labour movement was strong. The number of members of the associations of labour unions, FNV[7] and CNV, was rising continually. However, the labour movement did not operate harmoniously; some of the constituent labour unions were rather militant. The militancy of the labour movement was the reason why in 1974 the MHP was established.[8] This association consisted of the unions for white collar workers. The reason for establishing the MHP was that the labour movement took a too radical position with regard to income redistribution. The white collar workers' unions felt that the emphasis of the policy of the labour movement was too much on the position of the blue collar workers (Reynaerts and Nagelkerke, 1986; Hemerijck, 1992).

In the 1960s, in a situation of tight labour markets, the employers' organizations had been willing to accept rising wages. In the 1970s, however, the response to the increased militancy of the labour movement was much firmer. The employers found themselves in strong opposition with the labour movement (Wolinetz, 1989). Thus, the polarization between the political parties is reflected in the relation between the labour movement and the employers' organizations. This is the starting point for political economic interaction during the Den Uyl government.

In the next section the description of Dutch political economic interaction is limited to the time frame 1973-1998. It is standard practice for comparative political economic research to start the investigation at the beginning of the 1970s, for one of the main questions is how political actors reacted to the economic crisis of 1973-1974 and to the resulting changes in international economic relations. Another reason for starting the analysis in 1973 are the changes of the Dutch political system. As described, at the end of the 1960s depillarization and polarized political relations had changed the political game. Political parties had to adapt their strategies to a more open political system to attract voters. For the labour movement and the employers' organizations the new wage act

---

[7] The former associations of labour unions, the NVV and the NKV, merged into the FNV in 1976.

[8] MHP: Federation of Labour Unions for White Collar Workers (*Vakcentrale voor Middelbaar en Hoger Personeel*).

implied changing political economic relations. The framework of the present chapter is developed to describe the interactions between the political actors as they occur in this new situation. Because the first two governments at the beginning of the 1970s did not complete their term of office it seems reasonable to start the analysis with Cabinet Den Uyl. Hence, the description of Dutch political economic interaction on the basis of the analytical framework begins in 1973.

4.4 Institutional Interaction in the Netherlands[9]

Cabinet Den Uyl (1973-1977)

With a strong labour movement and a government dominated by left-wing ministers the conditions for a political exchange according to corporatist rules appear to be present. In terms of the theoretical framework the left-wing government would prefer to turn left. In exchange for wage restraint it would follow Keynesian demand management policies to boost employment and it would employ policies improving the income distribution in favour of the lower income groups. The policies proposed by the Den Uyl government indeed contained measures aimed at income redistribution. In 1974 the minimum wage as well as all social security benefits were indexed to average private sector wage increases (Visser, 1992).[10]

Table 4.1 presents the essential political economic figures of the Den Uyl government. At first sight this table may make a disorderly impression. However, the intention is that the design of the table illustrates the two possible games political actors can play. On the left-hand side of the table the left-wing goals and the labour movement

---

[9] This section relies heavily on the following literature: Visser (1990, 1992), Hemerijck (1992, 1994a), Wolinetz (1989) and Albeda (1994). Many institutional facts important for analysing Dutch political economic interaction were already described in this literature.

[10] The old age benefits were already linked, on a net basis, to the minimum wage in 1969. In 1974 the other minimum social security benefits were on a net basis linked to the minimum wage. The benefits above minimum level remained indexed to the wage level on a gross basis (Van der Hoek, 1996).

variables are presented; on the right-hand side are the right-wing goals and a variable indicating the behaviour of the employers. Presented at the top and the bottom of the table are the political parties forming the government. The growth of world trade is presented in this table as an indicator of international economic developments.

The Den Uyl government was serious about income redistribution, which is shown by the figures in table 4.1.[11] From 1974 until 1977 there was a rise in income of 6.5% for the *modal* income category, whereas the income of the category *minimum plus* increased by 8.9%. Total social security spending as a percentage of net national income increased by 6.4 percentage points. These figures demonstrate that the Den Uyl government attached much importance to incomes policy (especially if compared to the results of later governments).

Regarding other economic results, the following (cumulatative) figures for this government are of importance. Unemployment increased by 3.1 percentage points, as opposed to 2.2 percentage points for the European Community. The price index increased by 51%; in the EC it increased by 79%. With regard to public finance, the government deficit rose by 3.3 percentage points, taxation as a percentage of national increased by 1.1 percentage points and, finally, total government spending as a percentage of national income rose by 3.9 percentage points. Rising unemployment and public finance problems - despite higher natural gas revenues - may be explained by the crisis in the international economy - a crisis that was triggered by the oil crisis of 1973.

---

[11] The data used in this section stem from the same sources as the data used in previous chapters, namely OECD, CPB and CBS. Data which were not used earlier are explained at the bottom of the table. The figures on income policies are calculated on the basis of CPB-data; the bureau started to report data on income distribution in 1974.

Table 4.1   Cabinet Den Uyl, 1973-1977. A turn to the left?

	PvdA	D66	PPR	CDA[12]
seats in 1973	43	6	7	41

to the left			*to the right*		
incomes policy	total	yearly average	fiscal policy	total	yearly average
MODAL	+6.5%	+1.6%	GOVDEF	+3.3%-pts	+0.7%-pts
MINIMUM-PLUS	+8.9%	+2.2%	TAX	+1.1%-pts	+0.2%-pts
			GOVSP	+3.9%-pts	+0.8%-pts
MINIMUM	n.a.				
SOCSEC	+6.4%-pts	+1.3%-pts			
unemployment			inflation		
URNL	+3.1%-pts	+0.6%-pts	INFLNL	+51%	+8.6%
UREC	+2.2%-pts	+0.4%-pts	INFLEC	+79%	+12.3%

LABOUR			EMPLOYERS		
MEMBERS	+178000	+35600	EMPL	-4.5%	-1.1%
LIS	+8.1%-pts	+1.6%-pts			

	world trade	total	yearly average
	WORLD	+28.2%	+5.2%

	PvdA	D66	PPR	CDA[13]
seats in 1977	53	8	3	49

MODAL: change in income of modal income category (CPB)
MINIMUM PLUS: change in income of income category on, or just above, minimum wage level (CPB)
MINIMUM: change in income of income category with minimum social security benefits (CPB)
LIS: Labour Income Share, including income ascribed to the self-employed (CPB)

---

[12] The two confessional parties in this government were the ARP and the KVP. With the CHU these parties formed the CDA at the end of the 1970s.

[13] Electoral outcome for the CDA, including the CHU.

The question is how the government responded to this crisis. Apart from mandatory wage controls in 1974 and in 1976 (Visser, 1990), the government initially responded to the crisis in the world economy by Keynesian spending programmes (Fortuyn, 1983). It was especially Prime Minister Den Uyl (PvdA) and Minister of Social Affairs Boersma (ARP) who wanted to beat rising unemployment by extra government spending (Toirkens, 1988). However, soon the strategy changed in favour of the advocates of austerity programmes. It was Minister of Finance Duisenberg (PvdA) who in 1977 instigated the so-called 1%-measure, implying that the collective sector expenditures were not allowed to increase more than 1% of net national income a year.

In 1973 the Den Uyl government started with an ambitious left-wing political programme. Despite the international economic crisis it succeeded in bringing about a more equal income distribution. Unemployment, however, rose faster than it did in the rest of Europe, despite the fact that economic growth in the Netherlands was higher than OECD growth (Fortuyn, 1983; Therborn, 1986). The government started the term in a Keynesian way, but it changed to monetarist policies to cope with problems of rising public expenditures. According to some authors, notably Therborn, unemployment could have been lower had the government given priority to fighting unemployment. However, despite the fact that unemployment is generally seen as a left-wing political objective, it may be maintained that the government partly complied with its end of the corporatist exchange with the labour movement by following income redistribution policies.

After the struggle about the wage act of 1970, which was part of the intended decentralization of Dutch industrial relations, the labour movement became more radical. Despite the return to free collective bargaining in the 1960s, wage policy remained a matter of consultation between the centralized labour movement, the employers' organizations and the government (Wolinetz, 1989). However, reaching central agreements between these political actors proved to become a difficult matter in the 1970s. The radicalized labour movement, in which the central federations lost their hold on the unions and the rank and file of the unions, leading to, for example, wild cat strikes in the early 1970s, demanded income redistributing policies. The only central agreement of the 1970s was arranged for 1973. In the agreement the government and the central organizations of labour and employers agreed on the distribution of the growth of national income. Income redistribution (by means of a degressive distribution of the compensation for price increases) was part of the agreement (Windmuller, De Galan and Van Zweeden, 1983).

The oil crisis of 1973 and a deterioraton of the international economic situation hampered the realization of central agreements during the Den Uyl government. The government responded to the international crisis with mandatory wage controls. However, in exchange for income redistribution and expansive fiscal policies the labour movement accepted a mandatory wage control at the end of 1973 (Hemerijck, 1994a; Visser, 1992). Moreover, the government explicitly sought the cooperation of labour to cope with the economic crisis. 'Since it [the government] saw the support of its trade union allies rather than the cooperation of employers as the key to success, these controls were packaged in policies aiming at income redistribution, expansion and individualization of the family-based social security system and job-creation programme' (Visser, 1992: 341).

The question to be answered is whether wage increases were really moderated. The rise of the labour income share (*LIS*) of 8.1 percentage points in the four years of the Den Uyl government does not point in that direction. The problem in the 1970s, according to some authors, seems to have been that there was no success in commanding a general wage moderation (Visser, 1992; Van Riel, 1995). Rising wages in the low paid sector (the sheltered services sector) meant a pressure on the wages in the international high paid sector. With a deterioration of international competitiveness, due to the appreciation of the guilder,[14] it was impossible for the international sector to pass on higher wages by increasing prices (Van Riel, 1995). In other words, the international sector of the Netherlands fell into a profit squeeze situation despite efforts to control wage increases. Thus, despite wage moderation imposed by the government, labour costs were too high and profits fell. At the same time the radicalized unions turned against the institutions of central consultation, which limited the room for negotiations for their representatives (Hemerijck, 1994a). In sum, the labour movement did not really act in a cooperative way, although it did sympathise with the centre-left government. The Dutch labour movement in the first half of

---

[14] The appreciation of the guilder is explained by the exports of natural gas and by the linking of the guilder to the D-mark. The Dutch Central Bank (DNB) pursued restrictive monetary policies.

the 1970s was too radicalized to make it possible on a central level to really agree on wage moderation. This conclusion contradicts the corporatist model, which expects cooperative behaviour from the labour movement when a left-wing government is in power.

The employers' organizations resisted the radicalizing labour movement and opposed to the government policies of income redistribution. They also disagreed with the Keynesian policy reaction to the economic crisis in 1974. In an open letter to Prime Minister Den Uyl nine presidents of the largest Dutch corporations criticized the policies of the Social Democratic-dominated government and demanded a more restrictive financial government policy and wage moderation (Koole and Therborn, 1987; Visser, 1992). According to Visser (1992: 341) this 'vote of no-confidence' materialized in a decline of domestic investments and increasing investments overseas by Dutch corporations. Calculated on the basis of CPB-data it can be shown that employment in the market sector declined by 4.5% during the Den Uyl government.

Apart from the employers and employers' organizations it was the Central Planning Bureau and the Dutch Central Bank who urged for austerity with regard to government expenditures (Therborn, 1986; Koole and Therborn, 1987; Fortuyn, 1983). Consequently, the pressure on the government to change its Keynesian policy increased. Toirkens (1988) described how in the cabinet the ministers who favoured austerity measures - notably Minister of Finance Duisenberg (PvdA) - indeed caught the upper hand. With rising inflation, increasing unemployment and foreseeable financial problems for the government the cabinet seemed to have had no choice than to abandon Keynesian policies. Whereas the labour unions did not agree with this policy shift, the employers were of the opinion that the austerity measures (Duisenberg's 1%-policy rule) were not enough. In 1976 the relations between the cabinet and the social partners began to deteriorate seriously (Windmuller, De Galan and Van Zweeden, 1983).

This scenario resembles the scenario predicted by Scharpf's model (1987, 1991). Scharpf assumed that the behaviour of unions is solely determined by short term economic self-interest. In a situation where unemployment is not (yet) sharply increasing, unions will have an incentive to shift from a cooperative strategy to an aggressive one and demand higher wages. If labour unions do not moderate wage demands, it is difficult for left-wing governments to pursue ideological goals. In a situation of international crisis and the danger of accelerating inflation -

cost push inflation, due to rising oil prices - Scharpf predicted that left-wing governments will shift from Keynesian policies to monetarist policies if the labour movement does not cooperate by moderating wage claims.[15]

Scharpf's model predicted that if government policy remained expansive, while the unions demanded higher wages, a Labour government would be in an awkward political position. With rising inflation the middle group of voters would shift its vote to a right-wing government. On the other hand, the switch to a monetarist policy would worsen the situation (very high unemployment, high inflation), *unless* the unions could be persuaded by such a policy to moderate wage demands again. With a monetarist policy and moderate wage claims of the unions the electoral position would be safe again. According to Scharpf such a strategy gambles on the short-term reaction of the labour unions, but it is the only strategy that may raise the electoral chances of left-wing governments. So far this is in line with the Dutch scenario. The switch to a monetarist policy is in accordance with Scharpf's model. To some degree this policy shift prevented the Netherlands from ending up in a situation of very high inflation, although probably at the cost of some unemployment. Because unemployment was not extremely high, although rising, and because there was an expected chance of very high inflation, the policy shift of a centre-left government was rational because in this situation the middle group of voters prefer policies aimed at fighting inflation instead of Keynesian policies to create extra employment. However, according to Scharpf's model the electoral beneficiary of this policy shift should have been the Christian Democrats and not the Social Democrats. Although their strategy was rational, it should have led to an electoral victory only if the labour movement had responded by shifting to a cooperative strategy. By 1977 that was not the case yet. Consequently, Scharpf's model cannot explain the electoral victory of the Social Democrats.

The electoral consequences for the PvdA of their policy shift indeed were far from disappointing. The Social Democrats won ten seats in

---

[15] Scharpf admitted that his model cannot explain why in some countries, such as Austria and Brittain, labour unions followed a cooperative strategy in the mid-1970s. For a critical discussion of Scharpf's model, including some extra empirical evidence for other countries than the four Scharpf examined, see also Kitschelt (1994).

parliament which was a historical victory. The party went from 43 to 53 seats. The Liberal Democrats (D66) also gained; they went from six to eight seats. According to Scharpf's model and the assumption that the middle group of voters is the core constituency of the CDA, it should have been the Christian Democrats who should have won the election. However, the CDA did not gain much; the electoral results in 1977 were comparable with the results for the Christian Democratic parties in 1972. Finally, the PPR, the most leftist party of the government lost four seats in parliament; it fell from seven to three.

Cabinet Van Agt I (1977-1981)

After the election of 1977 it took 208 days to form a new cabinet. It seemed logical that a new government would consist of the party that won the election, namely the PvdA. However, the protracted negotiations between the PvdA and the, by then formed, CDA failed on the appointment of ministers for the new cabinet. The Christian Democrats took over the initiative and in a short period of time Cabinet Van Agt I was formed, consisting of the CDA and the VVD. Its programme was based on the policies of the previous government, namely to get the public sector under control, fight inflation and increase employment. It made it difficult for the PvdA to play its role as opposition party in parliament (Fortuyn, 1983).[16]

In comparison with the previous government the goals of the Van Agt Cabinet shifted to typical right-wing ones such as fighting inflation and reducing the deficit. However, the government was not prepared to take drastic austerity measures and did not choose for a clear-cut right-wing policy perspective.[17] For example, it did not want to abolish automatic price compensation and to disconnect social security benefits from private sector wages. The success of its policies to decrease public sector expenditures and to lower the government deficit therefore depended on the moderation of wage claims by the labour movement

---

[16] According to Kitschelt (1994) the failure of the PvdA to form a cabinet in 1977 was politically irrational. The politically strong position it had was destroyed for many years to come.

[17] According to Knoester (1988) the policies of the Van Agt I cabinet were a mixture of Keynesian and neo-classical and monetarist ideas.

(Hemerijck, 1994a). In other words, the government wanted the cooperation of the labour movement. In terms of the theoretical framework, this government neither chose to turn left, nor right.

Table 4.2   Cabinet Van Agt I, 1978-1981. A turn to the right?

	CDA	VVD			
seats in 1977	49	28			

to the left			*to the right*		
incomes policy	total	yearly average	fiscal policy	total	yearly average
MODAL	-3.5%	-0.9%	GOVDEF	+4.0%-pts	+1.0%-pts
MINIMUM-	-1.1%	-0.3%	TAX	+0.1%-pts	+0.0%-pts
PLUS			GOVSP	+3.9%-pts	+0.8%-pts
MINIMUM	-1.9%	-0.6%			
SOCSEC	+4.0%-pts	+1.0%-pts			
unemployment			inflation		
URNL	+3.0%-pts	+0.8%-pts	INFLNL	+23%	+5.4%
UREC	+2.7%-pts	+0.7%-pts	INFLEC	+55%	+11.5%

LABOUR			**EMPLOYERS**		
MEMBERS	+14000	+3500	EMPL	-1.4%	-0.4%
LIS	+4.0%-pts	+1.0%-pts			

	world trade	total	yearly average
	WORLD	+19.5%	+4.6%

	CDA	VVD
seats in 1981	48	26

The government set out to convince the labour movement to moderate wage claims and hoped that wage moderation would alleviate public finance problems and stimulate employment. In the theoretical framework this means that the government at the same time wanted to pursue a monetarist policy to lower inflation and taxation, but also a corporatist exchange with the labour movement by promising employment and balanced income developments in exchange for wage moderation. However, due to worsening international economic circumstances (the second oil crisis of 1979) and rising public debt, it had not much to offer in exchange for wage restraint (Visser, 1990). Instead of offering social security policies and policies aimed at income redistribution, the government hoped to satisfy the labour movement with legislation for the work councils, health and safety legislation and proposals to limit higher incomes - all measures that were already part of the political discussion during the previous government (Wolinetz, 1989; Visser, 1990).

The wavering position of the government was represented by the conflicting relations between two Christian Democratic ministers, namely Albeda, Minister of Social Affairs and Andriessen, Minister of Finance (Toirkens, 1988; Hemerijck, 1994a). Albeda stressed the importance of the cooperation of the labour movement and the employers' organizations to fight rising unemployment. Cuts in government expenditures were necessary, but had to be made acceptable for the labour movement. By offering unemployment programmes, income redistribution, tax cuts, and so forth, Albeda hoped to convince the labour movement to voluntarily moderate wage demands. Lower wage increases were important for the government budget because of the direct connections between private sector wages, the wages in the public sector and the social security benefits. Andriessen, who opposed Albeda's efforts to maintain good relations with the labour movement, wanted more radical austerity measures to control the budget deficit. Pressurized by the Dutch Central Bank to lower the deficit, and regularly confronted with gloomy expectations projected by the Central Planning Bureau he time and again proposed drastic austerity measures and wage freezes. Because of lack of support in both the cabinet and parliament Andriessen resigned in 1980 (Toirkens, 1988; Hemerijck, 1994a).

The labour movement was not eager to give up wage indexation, but it was willing to moderate wage demands in exchange for job preservation agreements and reduction of working time (Wolinetz, 1989). Rising unemployment figures weakened the political position of the labour movement, although total membership of the FNV, the CNV and the MHP still rose by 14,000 during Van Agt's period of government. Despite the fact that the political position of the labour movement weakened and despite the willingness to moderate wage demands, the labour income share rose by 4.0 percentage points, indicating that there were no drastic interventions in the process of wage formation. Consequently, the hope of the government for moderate wage increases seems to have been in vain.

The employers and their organizations welcomed the fact that a centre-right cabinet took control of government, but wanted more drastic austerity measures. The detached attitude of employers may have been one of the reasons for the disappointingly low level of investments which led to a decline of employment in the market sector of 1.4% in four years. In contrast, world trade increased by 19.5% in four years, a yearly average growth of 4.6%.

Following Knoester (1988), and looking at the results in table 4.2, it may be concluded that the economic policies of Cabinet Van Agt I failed. There was no internal agreement in the cabinet about the political way to reach economic goals. There were some austerity measures - in 1978 the austerity plan *Blueprint 1981* was published (Visser, 1990) - there were also some mandatory wage controls, but there was never unanimity over a complete set of either Keynesian or monetarist measures to deal with increasing unemployment and mounting public finance problems. Unemployment increased by 3 percentage points, compared to 2.7 percentage points for the European Community, and there was an average yearly inflation of 5.4% (in the EC it was 11.5%). So, with respect to inflation the Netherlands performed better than average in Europe, but unemployment did not decline as was promised by the government.

With respect to public finance the following cumulative figures are calculated. The deficit rose by 4 percentage points. The tax ratio did not change much (+ 0.1 percentage points), whereas total government spending increased by 3.7 percentage points. Income of the *modal* income category declined by 3.5 percentage points; *minimumplus* declined by 1.1 percentage points and *minimum* by 1.9 percentage points. Total social security expenditures, however, increased by 4 percentage points. In conclusion, the social economic policies of this cabinet were a complete failure. The public finance situation did not improve, but deteriorated instead. Unemployment did not decline, it increased. Inflation remained fairly high, although not as high as for the European Community. The question is whether these poor economic results affected the outcome of the 1981 general election. It is clear that Cabinet Van Agt I was not ready to choose to turn right in terms of the theoretical framework. According to Scharpf's model, in a situation of high unemployment and rather high inflation rates, such a choice would have been a rational strategy to raise electoral chances.

At first sight the electoral consequences appear to be limited to a small loss of seats in parliament. The VVD lost two seats and the CDA only one. However, the coalition lost its majority in parliament as a consequence of which the government coalition of Conservative Liberals and Christian Democrats could not be continued. For the PvdA the failure to form a cabinet in 1977 and the unsuccessful opposition role led to a loss of nine seats (Van Mierlo, 1981). However, whereas in 1977 an electoral victory did not lead to participation in government, the political circumstances in 1981 - despite the electoral loss - did lead to government participation. This is explained by the pivotal role played by D66. The PvdA preferred a coalition cabinet of left-wing parties, but accepted as a second best solution the unavoidable cooperation with the CDA (and D66). Therefore, the formation of a new coalition government depended on the coalition preference of D66. This political party expressed a clear preference for a coalition with the PvdA and the CDA as opposed to a coalition with the VVD and the CDA (Van Mierlo, 1981; Toirkens, 1988).

Cabinets Van Agt II and III (1981-1982)

Considering the polarized relations between the PvdA and the VVD there was only one feasible coalition after the election of 1981, namely the one with the CDA, the PvdA and D66. In the new government the PvdA and the CDA both had six ministers and D66 only three. Van Agt (CDA) became Prime Minister, whereas former Prime Minister Den Uyl became Minister of Social Affairs. The two principal goals of this cabinet were to reduce the deficit by economizing on public expenditures and, at the same time, to reduce unemployment. Regarding the latter, Den Uyl even changed the name of his department into the department of Social Affairs and Employment (Hemerijck, 1994a). Other leading persons in the cabinet were Van der Stee (CDA) as Minister of Finance, Van Thijn (PvdA) as Minister of Domestic Affairs and D66 leader Terlouw as Minister of Economic Affairs.

Table 4.3   Cabinets Van Agt II and III, 1982. A turn to the left?

		PvdA	D66	CDA		
seats in 1981		44	17	48		

to the left				*to the right*		
incomes policy	total			fiscal policy	total	
MODAL	-2.2%			GOVDEF	+1.7%-pts	
MINIMUM-	-1.4%			TAX	-0.9%-pts	
PLUS				GOVSP	+0.9%-pts	
MINIMUM	-2.2%			CTB	+0.3%-pts	
SOCSEC	+0.4%-pts			CE	+1.2%-pts	
unemployment				inflation		
URNL	+2.9%-pts			INFLNL	+5.4%	
UREC	+1.3%-pts			INFLEC	+11.0%	

LABOUR				**EMPLOYERS**		
MEMBERS	+17000			EMPL	-3.9%	
LIS	-0.3%-pts					

		world trade	total			
		WORLD	+1.4%			

		PvdA	D66	CDA		
seats in 1982		47	6	45		

CTB: Collective Tax Burden in % of gross domestic product (CPB)
CE: Collective Expenditures in % of gross domestic product (CPB)[18]

Whereas the political discussion in the previous cabinet had been dominated by two Christian Democrats - the Minister of Finance against

---

[18] Since the 1980s the variables CTB and CE have played an important role in Dutch economic discussions. In contrast to TAX and GOVSP, these variables incorporate social security spending and national insurance contributions.

the Minister of Social Affairs - the discussions regarding economic goals and policies now were guided by the differences of opinion between the three political parties. The CDA, especially personified by Van der Stee, gave priority to reducing the deficit, whereas the PvdA emphasized the importance of employment policies. D66 took the middle position in both policy areas. The differences of opinion between the political parties led to a discordant coalition. In terms of the analytical framework this cabinet, as the previous one, neither chose to turn left, nor right.

Den Uyl claimed four or five billion guilders for his employment programme, whereas Finance Minister Van der Stee only wanted to spend 300 million. The Christian Democrats wanted to cut 4.5 billion in government spending, whereas the Social Democrats did not want to go further than 2.5 billion. D66 again took the middle position by aiming at an amount of three or four billion guilders (Toirkens, 1988). The PvdA opposed drastic measures in the field of social security. Neither did the Social Democrats want to disconnect the social security benefits and the public sector wages from the development of the private sector wages. However, Den Uyl was prepared to accept a cut in the sickness benefits - social security benefits for sick employees - to save his employment programme (Hemerijck, 1994a). Both employers and the labour unions strongly objected to this cut. Den Uyl had hoped to exchange a cut in sickness benefits for employment, but due to the resulting strikes Den Uyl had to abandon this plan. According to Hemerijck the conflict between Den Uyl and the labour unions implied that a centre-left cabinet no longer guaranteed the support of the labour movement for a corporatist exchange (Hemerijck, 1992). Because the ministers of the PvdA would not accept further proposals for cuts in government spending - proposals which came especially from Finance Minister Van der Stee - they soon resigned and the cabinet fell in the spring of 1982 after it had been in office for only a few months.

Consisting only of ministers from D66 and the CDA Cabinet Van Agt III continued to attend to matters and to prepare the national budget for 1983. In September 1982 - after the general election - this government was even the first cabinet to propose cuts in public sector incomes and thus disregarding the automatic mechanisms that connected public sector incomes to market wages. However, a new cabinet was about to be formed and Cabinet Van Agt III knew that it did not have to impose the proposed measures (Hemerijck, 1992).

The economic results in 1982 were very poor. The Christian Democrats had meant to reduce the public deficit, whereas the Social Democrats had hoped to lower unemployment. The reverse came true: unemployment increased by 2.9 percentage points and the government deficit rose by 1.7 percentage points. It was expected that the PvdA would suffer a considerable loss in the election. This expectation did not materialize. On the contrary, there was even a small gain of three seats in parliament, whereas the Christian Democrats lost three. Considering the failure of this cabinet's term of office it is not surprising that the election led to a significant victory for the Conservative Liberals (VVD). They gained ten seats. D66 was the loser; it lost eleven of its seventeen seats in parliament. The major consequence of the 1982 election was that the Christian Democrats and the Conservative Liberals again attained a parliamentary majority (81 out of 150 seats) which paved the road for the first cabinet led by Lubbers (Gladdish, 1983).

Cabinets Lubbers I and II (1982-1989)

'In the early 1980s the economic and political climate rapidly deteriorated, preparing the ground for more drastic cures. ... Both employers and unions had grown tired of government intervention. The ultimate proof of ineffectiveness was delivered by the quarrelsome centre-left coalition, which once again curtailed bargaining power but could not deliver on employment' (Visser, 1990: 213). This was indeed the point of departure for the Lubbers Cabinets which dominated Dutch politics during the 1980s. On the one hand the effect was that, in terms of the theoretical framework, these cabinets clearly opted to turn right. On the other hand it led the social partners - more or less independent of the government - to make bipartite agreements about wages and employment.

With respect to the first notion, the central objectives of Cabinet Lubbers I, which consisted of eight Christian Democratic ministers and six Conservative Liberal ones, were to reduce the deficit without raising taxes, to stimulate economic activity in the market sector and to reduce unemployment. The emphasis was on the first objective (Toirkens, 1988). In the corporatist structure of Dutch economic policy it had been customary that the government based its social economic policies on serious consultation with the social partners in the SER. Because of ongoing conflicts within the labour movement, the inability to make social agreements between the social partners and the failure of the SER to provide the government with unanimous advice, the 'no nonsense' Cabinet Lubbers turned to technocratic advisory commissions (Hemerijck, 1994a). This is illustrated by the fact that the right-wing proposals of the Lubbers Cabinet were inspired by the Wagner Commission. Under the direction of Royal Dutch Shell's chief executive Wagner this advisory commission in 1981 and 1982 published two reports containing proposals to stimulate re-industrialization in the Netherlands (Visser, 1990; Wolinetz, 1989). Visser (1990: 213) enumerated the following recommendations: the government should distance itself from collective bargaining, all automatisms should be removed (cost-of-living-adjustments, minimum wages, linkage for social benefits and public service salaries), the minimum wage should be lowered and income differentials should be enlarged.

The government indeed eliminated the linkage between private and public sector wages. In 1983 public sector wages and social security benefits were cut back by 3% (Albeda, 1987, 1994). Toirkens (1988) stressed that there was not always unanimity in the cabinet regarding the austerity measures. During the government's term of office financial and economic objectives had to be readjusted regularly. However, after the attempts of the Van Agt Cabinets, this cabinet was the first to succeed in its austerity objectives. Moreover, Cabinet Lubbers I was the cabinet that abolished Keynesian policy in the Netherlands (Knoester, 1989). With the reduction of the deficit as the primary objective of structural economic policy the monetarist idea was, according to Knoester, that reducing the deficit would create room for private sector investments (less crowding out). In addition, income differences were widened and profits increased. From 1983 until 1986 the budget deficit decreased by 3 percentage points without increasing taxation, indicating that public spending actually was reduced (in relation to the growth of national income). *Modal* income slightly decreased by 0.9% (a yearly average of -0.2%). In contrast, however, the income category *minimumplus* decreased by 1.3% and *minimum income* even by 5.4%, indicating that this cabinet really brought an end to income redistribution. The price index increased by 8.6% in four years (a yearly average inflation of only 2.2%), whereas it rose by 28.3% (a yearly average of 6.5%) in the EC-countries. The unemployment level remained high, although it was reduced by 1.5 percentage points (in comparison, unemployment in the EC-countries rose by 1.4 percentage points).

Table 4.4   Cabinet Lubbers I, 1983-1986. A turn to the right?

			CDA	VVD	
seats in 1982			45	36	

to the left			*to the right*		
incomes policy	total	yearly average	fiscal policy	total	yearly average
MODAL	-0.9%	-0.2%	GOVDEF	-3.0%-pts	-0.8%-pts
MINIMUM-PLUS	-1.3%	-0.3%	TAX	+0.0%-pts	+0.0%-pts
			GOVSP	-0.4%-pts	-0.1%-pts
MINIMUM	-5.4%	-1.4%	CTB	-0.6%-pts	-0.2%-pts
SOCSEC	-2.9%-pts	-0.7%-pts	CE	-2.8%-pts	-0.7%-pts
unemployment			inflation		
URNL	-1.5%-pts	-0.4%-pts	INFLNL	+8.6%	+2.2%
UREC	+1.4%-pts	+0.4%-pts	INFLEC	+28.3%	+6.5%

LABOUR			**EMPLOYERS**		
MEMBERS	-172000	-43000	EMPL	+2.0%	+0.5%
LIS	-9.1%-pts	-2.3%-pts			

	world trade	total	yearly average
	WORLD	+19.6	+4.8%

	CDA	VVD
seats in 1986	54	27

Apart from the fundamental changes in the social economic policies of the Netherlands during the 1980s, the most striking feature is, according to Wolinetz (1989: 95), 'the relatively autonomous role of the government in determining policy'. The labour movement initially protested against the austerity measures of the cabinet. However, the political position of the labour movement was too weak to successfully revolt against these measures. Unemployment was very high and union membership was decreasing: from 1983 until 1986 the labour unions lost 172,000 members. Under pressure of the cabinet and of the high unemployment rates, the employers' organizations and the labour movement came to a historical bipartite social agreement in the Foundation of Labour - the so-called Agreement of Wassenaar. This agreement contained proposals to renegotiate collective agreements (*CAOs*) to revoke automatic price compensation in exchange for reducing labour time and the stimulation of part-time work (Hemerijck, 1994a). With reference to this social agreement Albeda (1994) speaks about a fresh start for the Labour Foundation, because following this agreement more were to come in the 1980s and 1990s. Despite the voluntarily character of the social agreements, the labour income share in national income shows that there was at least a fairly moderate development of wages: the labour income share decreased by 9.1 percentage points in four years.[19] Visser (1992: 344) asserted that 'in the market sector, 1982 to 1986 was a period of wage moderation - a standstill in real terms with very low inflation rates'. The restauration of confidence of employers in the economic policies of the government is expressed by the modest growth of employment in the market sector: 2% in four years.

The solo of the government in their social economic policies payed off electorally especially for the Christian Democrats. Although unemployment remained high, on the field of public finance the government appeared to have 'a solid record of management' (Gladdish, 1987: 115).[20] Moreover, the important austerity measures concerning incomes policy were taken early in the government's term of office and not just before the election. The CDA won nine seats in parliament. In contrast, the Conservative Liberals lost nine. This may be explained by the RSV-scandal - government grants to a private company in Rotterdam,

---

[19] The revision of the definition of the LIS in 1985 is taken into account. From 1982 until 1994 the adjusted time series is used.

[20] Visser and Wijnhoven (1990) wondered why in the 1980s conservative governments in Europe were not punished by the electorate for enduring mass unemployment. They concluded that these governments apparently succeeded in mitigating and making acceptable the problem of unemployment. Governments succeeded in shifting attention to other economic parameters, for example, employment, inflation and prosperity. Visser and Wijnhoven, referring to national voting research, stated that in the Netherlands the proportion of voters that considered unemployment as the most important national problem declined from 58% to 37% between 1982 and 1986.

named RSV - and a dogmatic stance on the issue of deploying cruise missiles in the Netherlands (Gladdish, 1987). Despite the fact that the PvdA also won, it was to be expected that the coalition of the VVD and the CDA, retaining their majority in parliament, would form the next cabinet to finish its job.[21]

The moderation of wage claims by the labour movement is in accordance with Scharpf's original model. Scharpf explained why at the end of the 1970s and the beginning of the 1980s unions were willing to moderate wage claims while conservative governments pursued monetarist policies. These governments allowed unemployment to increase to counter rising inflation. In such a situation unions have to moderate wage claims to defend existing employment; in other words, they do not have much of a choice. It does not even make a difference whether the labour movement is strong and centrally organized, as the corporatist model presupposes, or whether it is fragmented in small, decentralized unions.

Note that this assertion contradicts the theory of, for example, Alvarez, Garrett and Lange (1991), as discussed in chapter one. They hypothesized that the strategic policy choices of 'encompassing' labour unions depend on whether there is a left-wing or a right-wing government. In a situation with a left-wing government labour unions are prepared to moderate wage claims, whereas in situations with a right-wing government their wage claims will be more militant. With respect to the Netherlands there is no evidence for this hypothesis. On the contrary, it is precisely during the centre-right Cabinet Lubbers I that wage claims were moderated, which confirms Scharpf's assertion that during conservative governments pursuing monetarist policies the labour movement has to moderate wage claims to defend employment for their members (see also Van Riel, 1995).

Cabinet Lubbers II continued to take austerity measures. Insofar as changes in the social security system had not already started to take effect during the previous government the following alterations took place: the level of social security benefits for the unemployed was lowered from 80% to 70% of previous wages and the period of entitlement was shortened; sickness benefits were reduced from 80% to 75% of previous

---

[21] 'Let Lubbers finish his job' was the slogan on the election poster of the Christian Democrats.

wages; and disability allowances were scaled down to 70% of the minimum wage (Visser, 1992; Wolinetz, 1989).

Table 4.5 Cabinet Lubbers II, 1987-1989. Still going to the right?

			CDA	VVD	
seats in 1986			54	27	

to the left			*to the right*		
incomes policy	total	yearly average	fiscal policy	total	yearly average
MODAL	+4.8%	+1.6%	GOVDEF	-0.6%-pts	-0.2%-pts
MINIMUM-	+3.5%	+1.2%	TAX	+0.4%-pts	+0.1%-pts
PLUS			GOVSP	+1.3%-pts	+0.4%-pts
MINIMUM	+1.6%	+0.5%	CTB	-0.4%-pts	-0.1%-pts
SOCSEC	+0.2%-pts	+0.1%-pts	CE	-4.5%-pts	-1.5%-pts
unemployment			inflation		
URNL	-1.6%-pts	-0.5%-pts	INFLNL	+1.1%	+0.4%
UREC	-1.8%-pts	-0.6%-pts	INFLEC	+12.7%	+4.2%

LABOUR			**EMPLOYERS**		
MEMBERS	+55000	+18333	EMPL	+6.8%	+2.2%
LIS	-5.0%-pts	-0.6%-pts			

	world trade	total	yearly average	
	WORLD	+23.8%	+7.4%	

			CDA	VVD	
seats in 1989			54	22	

This cabinet did not complete its term of office. The direct reason was the disagreement between the VVD and the CDA over the National Environment Plan.[22] The real causes, however, ran deeper, as Wolinetz

---

[22] Regarding this plan, the coalition partners were not able to come to an agreement about the fiscal deductions of the costs of driving to work.

(1990) pointed out. The relations between the coalition partners had been deteriorating since 1982. The VVD had lost nine seats in the election of 1986, whereas the CDA had won nine. A large part of the loss of the Conservative Liberals formed the gain for the Christian Democrats (Gladdish, 1987). The harsh austerity measures had improved the financial situation of the public sector. At the end of the 1980s the deficit had been reduced and the Dutch economy, following the world economy, was in an upswing. Although unemployment remained high, the need for further austerity measures became less apparent (Wolinetz, 1990a). At the end of the 1980s the VVD was afraid of another electoral loss, whereas the CDA was already considering the possibility of forming a government with the PvdA.

Despite the tension between the two coalition partners the results of Cabinet Lubbers II were partly in accordance with its intentions. In its two years of government the deficit was further reduced by 0.6 percentage points, but despite the austerity measures total government spending went up again (1.3 percentage points), as did social security spending (0.2 percentage points). The inflation rate remained very low and unemployment slightly decreased. The growth of employment in the market sector was impressive (6.8%).

The social partners kept on discussing policy matters in the Labour Foundation. The bipartite social agreement of 1982 was followed by a series of comparable agreements during the 1980s (and 1990s). These agreements contained recommendations for specific problems: youth unemployment (1984, 1986), long term unemployment (1987, 1989), minimum wage (1988), part time work (1989), unemployment under foreigners (1990, 1992) and handicapped employees (1990) (Hemerijck, 1994a: 39). These recommendations were not binding agreements; industrial relations since 1982 have been characterized by decentralized collective bargaining. However, the intention of the social partners on a central level was to stimulate wage restraint in exchange for private investments and employment (Hemerijck, 1994a). Although, as Albeda stated, the board of the FNV was willing to return to a form of central control of wages, decentralized bargaining was favoured by the government, the employers' organizations as well as by the labour unions. Albeda further noted that although after 1985 the political strength of the labour movement began to grow again (because of a considerable growth of employment), this did not lead to unacceptable wage increases. On the contrary, the figures show that the labour share again decreased by 4.8

percentage points. In conclusion, 'the new pattern seems to have become: a central dialogue on legislative and policy matters with the Government, combined with decentralized bargaining' (Albeda, 1994: 258).

The VVD lost again in the election of 1989. The Liberals lost five seats in parliament, whereas the Christian Democrats retained their number of seats, namely 54, and remained the largest political party in parliament. The PvdA suffered a small loss of three seats and failed to reach its electoral objective to become the largest party. Although the coalition of CDA and VVD preserved their majority (76 of the 150 seats in parliament) the new cabinet, as expected, was formed by the CDA and the PvdA. Lubbers became Prime Minister, whereas PvdA leader Kok became Minister of Finance and Vice-Premier (Wolinetz, 1990a).

Cabinet Lubbers/Kok (1989-1994)

Cabinet Lubbers/Kok was a coalition between the Christian Democrats and the Social Democrats. It implied the return of the PvdA to government. The number of ministers was divided equally between the two parties, namely seven for the CDA and seven for the PvdA. As Albeda (1994: 264) stated, this coalition 'held out greater prospects for reaching an agreement with the social partners, especially with the trade union movement'. In terms of the theoretical framework of this chapter the question is whether the direction of policy shifted from turning right to turning left (*van rechtsom naar linksom*).

Albeda explained that soon after the formation of the cabinet indeed a central agreement was reached, which was called 'a common framework for policy' (*Gemeenschappelijk Beleidskader*). It was signed by the Prime Minister and the social partners, except for the MHP. This broad agreement 'declared that the parties wanted to intensify their joint efforts to further economic growth and to reduce unemployment, acknowledging the responsibility of the cabinet on the one hand and of the social partners in their 'free and decentralized' collective bargaining on the other' (Albeda, 1994: 264). In 1990 and 1991 the linkage system between private sector wages and the minimum wage and social security benefits was partially restored. In 1992 a new law on the linkage system became effective. With the exception of the public sector wages, which have been seperately negotiated since the 1980s, the mimimum wage and the social security benefits were linked to private sector wages on two conditions. These conditions were that the development of the private sector wages would be moderated sufficiently and that the number of persons entitled to social security benefits would not be rising in proportion to the working part of the population (Hemerijck, 1994a).[23] These conditions notwithstanding, it looked as if the government had turned left.

One of the most important policy problems the government and the social partners encountered was the steep rise in the number of people who came to receive disability benefits. It was feared that by the year 2000 one million people would receive such benefits. In 1990, on a meeting between the government and the social partners, who were in the process of negotiating another central agreement, the problem of the rising numbers of recipients of disability benefits was already on the agenda (Albeda, 1994). However, the announcement in the summer of 1991 of austerity measures to deal with this problem came as a surprise to the social partners, the media and the public. The proposals to shorten the length of time of benefits and to lower the levels caused a major conflict between the labour movement and especially the PvdA. After the austerity measures of the 1980s and the improving economic situation at the end of this decade the idea had been that there was no need for further austerity measures. The policy reversal regarding the disability benefits, however, showed that the political leaders felt that the welfare state needed further restructuring (Visser, 1992).

The central agreement between the social partners and the government did not keep wages from rising. In relation to the austerity measures of the cabinet this is not surprising. The growing power of the labour unions - membership went up by more than 200,000 members - became visible in the increasing labour income share: it increased by 1.2

---

[23] Because these conditions were not satisfied, the linkage system was not fully applied (see Hemerijck, 1994a). An interesting note from Albeda concerns the belief of all the political actors that the system of decentralized bargaining in the 1980s is a better condition to control wages than the system of central wage bargaining of the 1970s. 'The reasoning is that in the case of central bargaining both parties try to run as little risk as possible, and therefore trade unions will ask for higher wages increases. Observers then point to the development in the 1970s when proposed measures to freeze wages were 'amended' by negotiations between the trade unions and the Cabinet (this took place especially during the Den Uyl Cabinet in 1973-77). Moreover, they note the tendency on the part of the social partners to correct the wage freeze after its period of validity' (Albeda, 1994: 265).

percentage points. Had there not been an economic slowdown in 1993, the labour income share would have increased by more than 5 percentage points. Despite the economic slowdown in this year and despite the rising labour income share, employment in the market sector still rose by 5.2 percentage points and the economic performance of the Netherlands during this cabinet did not deviate much from the performance of the previous one.

Table 4.6   Cabinet Lubbers/Kok, 1990-1994. A turn to the left?

	PvdA	CDA
seats in 1989	49	54

to the left			*to the right*		
incomes policy	total	yearly average	fiscal policy	total	yearly average
MODAL	+3.3%	+0.7%	GOVDEF	-2.9%-pts	-0.6%-pts
MINIMUM-PLUS	+2.3%	+0.5%	CTB	-0.7%-pts	-0.1%-pts
			CE	-2.6%-pts	-0.5%-pts
MINIMUM	-1.1%	-0.2%			
SOCSEC	+1.4%-pts	+0.3%-pts			
unemployment			inflation		
URNL	+0.2%-pts	+0.0%-pts	INFLNL	+13.4%	+2.1%
UREC	+3.2%-pts	+0.6%-pts	INFLEC	+22.7%	+4.5%

LABOUR			**EMPLOYERS**		
MEMBERS	+202000	+40400	EMPL	+5.2%	+1.0%
LIS	+1.2%-pts	+0.2%-pts			

	world trade	total	yearly average
	WORLD	+20.1%	+4.0%

	PvdA	CDA
seats in 1994	37	34

URNL: standard unemployment rate in % for *15* countries of the European Community (CPB)
INFLEC: yearly change consumer price index in % for *15* countries of the European Community (CPB)

The performance of this cabinet may be summarized in the following cumulative figures. Total government spending was reduced (by 2.6 percentage points), as well as the government deficit (-2.9 percentage points) and the tax burden (*collectieve lastendruk* by 0.7 percentage points). Social security spending, however, increased by 1.4 percentage points. The unemployment level hardly changed, whereas European unemployment increased by 3.2 percentage points. The income of the higher income groups increased more than the income of the lower income groups. *Minimum income* even decreased by 1.1%.

The return of the Social Democrats to government did not involve a radical change in government policies, at least not in a left-wing direction. In other words, Cabinet Lubbers/Kok did not take a radical turn left in terms of the theoretical framework of this chapter. The central agreement made at the start of the cabinet period, had appeared to be a return to a system of corporatist consultation about macroeconomic policy. It had appeared that the solo of the government during the 1980s in determining macroeconomic policies had come to an end. Moreover, with the restoration of the linkage system the cabinet had appeared to take a turn to the left. However, the austerity measures regarding the disability benefits soon changed this direction. As a consequence of this shift the relationship between the PvdA and the labour movement was disturbed. In terms of the theoretical framework, Cabinet Lubbers/Kok held out the promise to take a turn to the left, but did not comply with this promise. In comparison with the 1970s it is remarkable that the confidence of the employers in the Dutch economy was not hurt by the return of the Social Democrats to government. Despite rising wages and an economic slowdown in 1993, employment in the market sector increased by 5.2%.

Perhaps the government had hoped that austerity measures taken early in its term of office, would not play a significant role at the next general election. However, the electoral consequences were enormous. Both the CDA and the PvdA suffered massive losses. The CDA went from 54 seats in parliament to 34, a loss of 20 seats. The PvdA lost 12 seats and went from 49 to 37 seats in parliament. The reason for the loss of the PvdA was the disappointment of voters with the further austerity measures taken by the cabinet. It is clear that the austerity measures regarding the disability benefits were neither ideologically nor electorally a rational policy choice for the Social Democrats. The loss for the CDA may be explained by the leadership crisis of this party (the announcement of Lubbers's retreat from national politics) and by the announcement that the social security system needed further reconstruction, for example regarding the benefits for the elderly. Anyhow, these dramatic electoral results led to the realization of a supposedly inconceivable coalition government, namely the present 'purple' coalition of the PvdA, the VVD and D66.

Cabinet Kok (1994-1998)

The purple coalition of the Social Democrats, the Social Liberals and the Conservative Liberals was realized because a two-party coalition was impossible and this coalition was the only one D66 wanted to support. It was an old wish of D66 to form a cabinet without the Christian Democrats. This purple coalition meant a historical compromise between two parties - the VVD and the PvdA - with really different ideas about social and economic policies and about the role of the government. The coalition parties made rigorous agreements about public expenditures, reducing the deficit and reducing taxes. An important objective of this government was to comply with the financial criteria of the European Economic and Monetary Union.

'Jobs, jobs, jobs' was the central slogan of this cabinet. Reducing taxes was the most important instrument to bring about wage moderation and to stimulate employment, but there were two other instruments that illustrate the compromise between the PvdA and the VVD. For the long-term unemployed the cabinet created subsidized jobs, which were called Melkert jobs, named after the Social Democratic minister of Social Affairs and Employment. The VVD advocated a proposal to allow long-term unemployed to work below the minimum wage. Thus both the Social Democrats and the Conservative Liberals formulated their ideological employment proposals in the government agreement.[24]

---

[24] The advantageous economic circumstances and the pressure of the parliament made the government in 1997 to withdraw the minimum wage proposal.

Table 4.7   Cabinet Kok, 1995-1998. Left or right?

			PvdA	D66	VVD
seats in 1994			37	24	31

to the left			*to the right*		
incomes policy	total	yearly average	fiscal policy	total	yearly average
MODAL	+3.3%	+0.8%	GOVDEF	-1.3%-pts	-0.3%-pts
MINIMUM-	+4.0%	+1.0%	CTB	-1.5%-pts	-0.4%-pts
PLUS			CE	-3.3%-pts	-0.8%-pts
MINIMUM	+1.9%	+0.5%			
SOCSEC	-1.9%-pts	-1.0%-pts			
(until 1996)					
unemployment			inflation		
URNL	-2.8%-pts	-0.7%-pts	INFLNL	+6.9%	+1.7%
UREC	-1.0%-pts	-0.3%-pts	INFLEC	+9.7%	+2.4%

LABOUR			**EMPLOYERS**		
MEMBERS	+98400	+24600	EMPL	+10.1%	+2.5%
LIS	-0.7%-pts	-0.2%-pts			

	world trade	total	yearly average
	WORLD	+27.5%	+6.9%

	PvdA	D66	VVD
seats in 1998	45	14	38

With respect to social security policies the government agreement entailed that no cuts would be made in the level and length of benefits. However, the political parties agreed on the privatization of parts of the social security system to make it more efficient. In 1996 the sickness scheme was privatized: sickness is no longer insured by the collective social security system, but employers can take out private insurance for their obligation to pay sick employees 70% of pay during the first year of sickness. After the first year the disability scheme applies. The cabinet also reached an agreement on a revision of the disability scheme that became effective in 1998. The new system includes differentiation of premiums and the possibility for employers to opt out of the public scheme and take out private insurance (CPB, 1997; OECD, 1998). In other words, without making cuts in the social security benefits, this cabinet went on reforming the welfare state by introducing financial incentives into the social security system. It was an important compromise between the PvdA and the VVD.

More fincancial incentives, more market discipline and less government interference were crucial aspects for many policies of this government, not only in the field of social security, but also in a number of other sectors (for example, public transport, electricity, mail and financial markets) (OECD, 1998). According to the opposition parties in parliament Cabinet Kok was a neo-liberal cabinet dominated by the ideological ideas of the VVD. However, at the same time the government tried to cope with problems of poverty and took some specific measures to raise the income of the poorest people, especially at the end of the government's term of office, just before the general election of 1998 (a political business cycle!). It is therefore difficult to classify this cabinet as a centre-left or a centre-right cabinet. The cabinet neither went left, nor right. Because of the favourable economic circumstances it was possible for the participating political parties to compromise on social and economic policies.

Of great significance is the fact that the ideas of the political actors about economic policies have changed since the 1980s, implicating that for the 1990s the relevance of Scharpf's model has diminished. Especially the different ideas about macroeconomic policies between left-wing and right-wing political parties are less important now than they were in the 1970s. One reason is the fact that all European governments have to take account of the financial criteria of the Economic and Monetary Union, which reduces the possibilities for macroeconomic policies. However, more important is the fact that since the 1990s especially the Social Democrats seem to have been attaching more importance to increasing labour participation than to policies to redistribute income, which explains the readiness of the PvdA to cooperate in reforming the social security system.[25] Adapting the social security system and specific labour market

---

[25] In the 1970s income redistribution was one of the most important policy objectives for Cabinet Den Uyl. For Cabinet Kok stimulating employment has become more important than increasing minimum income.

policies became far more important in stimulating employment than Keynesian macroeconomic policies (see also Visser and Hemerijck, 1997; Hemerijck and Van Kersbergen, 1997). This policy shift cannot be explained by Scharpf's model.

Since this governments' term of office the so-called Dutch model has been attracting international attention (Visser and Hemerijck, 1997; OECD, 1998). The economic success of the Dutch economy, especially since the economic slowdown of 1993, is attributed to the role of the employers' organizations and the labour movement in formulating economic policies in general and in causing wage moderation in particular. The credit for the Dutch model has to be put in perspective. It is remarkable to see that it is precisely this cabinet that wanted to reduce the role of the social partners in the process of economic policy-making. This cabinet wanted to reduce the role of the SER, the central institution of the Dutch model. This cabinet wanted to abolish the administative extension of sectoral wage agreements (CAOs). This cabinet wanted to change the act on the minimum wage. Although these intentions were not executed, they were part of the government agreement. Especially the labour movement strongly opposed these kinds of measures. In other words, it is exaggerated to speak about a Dutch model of consensus about economic policies exactly in this cabinet's term of office.

However, it is true that the policies of this cabinet to reduce taxes helped to moderate wage demands. And this specific strategy of Cabinet Kok is an important part of the success of the Dutch model. Despite the policy intentions of the government and despite the increasing power of the labour movement in a situation of favourable economic circumstances, the labour movement moderated wage demands.[26] This illustrates that there now seems to be a measure of consensus about the commitment to increase labour participation. Since the 1980s labour market policies have become more important in the Netherlands than direct income policies, not only for the political parties, but also for the labour movement. One example of this commitment is the legislation on flexibilisation of labour relations (relaxation of dismissal protection) in combination with more social security for workers without stable jobs. Because of the central agreement between the labour movement and the employers on 'Flexibility and Security', the government was able to propose such a

---

[26] In such a situation Scharpf's model expects higher wage demands from the labour movement.

compromise. The combination of social security reforms without cutting social security benefits, reducing the tax burden and the government deficit, and the moderation of wage demands explains the succes of the Dutch economy in recent years.

The economic results of Cabinet Kok are impressive, especially with respect to stimulating employment in the market sector: on average a yearly rise of 2.5%. Unemployment was reduced more than it was in the European Union, whereas Dutch inflation remained moderate. Reducing the deficit and reducing taxes were central objectives of Cabinet Kok. Both goals were achieved by cutting back on government expenditures. Because of the favourable conditions on the labour market the social security expenditures also decreased. The income of all income groups increased, with the lowest increase for the minimum income group. The fall in the labour income share shows the success of the policy of wage moderation.

Both the PvdA and the VVD claimed the good performance of the Dutch economy. Both parties won additional seats in the general election of 1998. D66, the third coalition partner, played a subordinate role in Cabinet Kok and was punished in the election for its invisibility in the government. D66 lost 10 of its 24 seats in parliament. Nevertheless, after the elections D66 was willing to support a second Cabinet Kok with the same coalition partners.

4.5 Conclusion

The objective of this chapter was to gain insight into the interaction between governments and the labour movement and the employers' organizations. Moreover, the intention was to demonstrate that a descriptive framework presents a more complete explanation of partisan goals and electoral motives than the political economic interaction models of the previous chapters. Inspired by the research of comparative political economy, which assumes that (the success of) government policies is dependent on the interaction between the various political actors, an analytical framework for the description of Dutch political interaction was constructed. The similarity between this framework and Scharpf's model is mainly to be found in the emphasis on the influence the labour movement is assumed to have on the policy choices of the government.

Two observations are of particular importance: the policy shift of the Den Uyl government and the wage moderation in the 1980s. As the vicissitudes of the Den Uyl Cabinet showed, international developments have a major impact on the small, open economy of the Netherlands. It is therefore difficult for Dutch governments to pursue independent policies. Moreover, governments are forced to react to international developments by adjusting their policies. This is what happened during the 1970s. The political and economic circumstances forced the Den Uyl Cabinet to abandon, to a certain extent, its Keynesian policies. Due to international economic circumstances the government, preferring Keynesian policies, was dependent on the wage policies of the labour movement. Because the labour movement was not able to control wage demands sufficiently, the government had to shift to monetarist policies. However, the (limited) austerity measures did not lead to the abandoning of direct income redistribution policies.

Neither Cabinet Den Uyl, nor the Cabinets Van Agt, drastically changed their income redistribution policies. Apparently, it was politically impossible to abolish the linkages between private sector wages, public sector wages and social security benefits. However, unemployment increased, even more than it did in surrounding countries, which is in contrast to the expectations of the partisan theory. Political interaction appeared to have resulted in Cabinet Den Uyl giving priority to income redistribution measures and not to employment policies. In the 1970s the left-wing way to stimulate employment failed because the government had no resources to spend on employment programmes. Moreover, private investment decreased during Cabinet Den Uyl, which amplified the economic problems. In sum, the economic circumstances in the 1970s and the political impossibility to adjust the income redistribution policies (one of the cornerstones of Cabinet Den Uyl) explains why the hypothesis of the partisan models that employment is boosted by left-wing governments was rejected in chapter three.

Contrary to the expectations of the partisan theory, the analysis of the present chapter demonstrates that employment was stimulated during the governments of Prime Minister Lubbers in the 1980s. The austerity measures of these governments apparently did not lead to higher unemployment. With the help of an upswing in the international economy, private investment and employment in the private sector were stimulated by the lower production costs for employers and, in general, by a higher confidence of employers in centre-right governments. Moreover, the moderate wage claims of the labour unions also benefited private sector investments. In conformance with the expectations of Scharpf's model, with a right-wing government executing deflationary policies, the labour movement moderated wage demands.

The description of political economic interaction in the present chapter provides an explanation for the failure of the partisan models to describe the political economic situation in the 1970s and 1980s. Due to changing international economic circumstances and the behaviour of the labour movement and the employers, the Den Uyl government did not choose to really fight unemployment, but stuck to its income redistribution policy. In contrast, the Lubbers governments in the 1980s chose to deal with inflation and public finance problems. Due to this policy and the wage moderation of the unions, private sector investments were stimulated. Apparently, the success of economic policies, Keynesian or monetarist, is subject to international economic circumstances and the behaviour of the labour movement and the employers' organizations. In other words, the models of the partisan theory erroneously neglect the institutional structure in which governments have to pursue their preferred partisan objectives.

Governments react to economic circumstances and to the behaviour of other political actors. Nevertheless, they do take account of the electoral consequences of their policies. The shift from Keynesian to monetarist policies of Cabinet Den Uyl was electorally rational in terms of Scharpf's framework. However, this shift was triggered by economic developments and the wage policies of unions. It was not a systematic use of economic policies, determined in advance, to maximize votes at the next election. The Cabinets Lubbers I and II pursued their policies more autonomously than other cabinets. Consequently, these governments had a better opportunity to create a political business cycle than other governments. The elections appeared to have influenced the timing of the policies of these governments. The austerity measures, which formed the heart of the policies of these cabinets, were taken at the beginning and during the government's term of office. In the last year before the elections governments were more cautious about cutting public expenditures. The same may apply for Cabinet Lubbers/Kok. Perhaps this cabinet had hoped that the measures regarding the disability benefits, announced rather early in the government's term of office, would have been forgotten at the election of 1994. Obviously, this has been a serious miscalculation of both the Social Democrats and the Christian Democrats.

In the case of cabinet Kok it is remarkable that many specific inome policies were implemented at the end of it's term of office, which indicates a kind of political business cycle as suggested by Tufte (1978). In sum, electoral motives obviously influence policy choices, but not as systematic as the models of the political business cycle assume. These models are far too mechanistic to describe the influence of electoral objectives.

Although the framework, based on Scharpf's model, does take account of institutional interaction and does explain why left-wing governments shifted from Keynesian to monetarist policies, it leaves many questions unanswered. The framework, for example, cannot explain the electoral victory for the PvdA in 1977, the policy shift of Cabinet Lubbers/Kok with respect to the disability benefits and the realization in 1994 of the coalition government of the PvdA, the VVD and D66. During Cabinet Kok's term of office the Dutch model attracted international attention. The key to the recent success of the Dutch model is the consensus about the commitment to increase labour market participation. But it is remarkable that it was especially this government that wanted to change the Dutch corporatist model of cooperation and consensus. The description of Dutch political economic interaction in this chapter illustrates that the Dutch model is not an unchanging reality. It develops under the influence of ideological policy choices and economic circumstances. It is clear that in the Netherlands on the national level of policy-making the role of the social partners is an important one, but it is not always of the same importance. The fact that it is precisely Cabinet Kok that wanted to change the model by reducing the influence of the social partners in the process of economic policy-making illustrates the instability of the Dutch model. If economic circumstances change, the consensus about economic policies may vanish and political relations may polarize again. It is not predictable what that would mean for the behaviour of the social partners and the social economic policies of the government.

Summary and Conclusion

The central question of this book was whether, and if so how, political motivations - electoral and ideological - influence economic policies and affect the economy in a capitalist democracy. Although there are many different scientific approaches to the study of the interaction between democratic politics and the economy, in this book only several theories were discussed. The models of the *political business cycle* and the *partisan theory* were taken as a starting-point for the discussion of the central question. Subsequently, the issue was whether the *institutional structure* in which political decisions are made, really enable parties or politicians to pursue ideological or opportunistic objectives. The various theories, presented and commented upon in chapter one, were classified into two broad categories, namely the *economics of politics* and the *politics of economics*. Although this classification has its shortcomings, it was used to stress the difference between political mechanisms and institutional structures. The economics of politics approach may be broadly regarded as an individualistic economic theory of politics, whereas the politics of economics approach stresses the importance of the social, historical and institutional context in which political economic interaction is taking place.

Part of the economics of politics approach are the *political business cycle* models which assume that politicians are only interested in getting re-elected. Assuming that voters cast their votes on the basis of economic outcomes, politicians employ economic policies in order to maximize their chances of being re-elected. Therefore, the manipulation of economic policies by opportunistic politicians results in political business cycles. These politicians' idea is to make the economy 'look good' around election time. This usually means that before an election the government expands public spending to stimulate economic growth and boost employment. The consequences of such policies, higher inflation for example, are left to be taken care of after the election. After the election the government is then forced to employ deflationary policies to control inflation, which may well cause unemployment.

Political business cycle models are mechanistic economic models. The development of political business cycle theory is related to the development of macroeconomic theory. These kinds of models succeeded in taking account of theoretical novelties. Initially based on monetarist theory, in time political business cycle models incorporated rational expectations and game theoretical refinements. But the assumed behaviour of politicians remained the same, namely to rationally maximize votes to win elections. In this book it is argued that this interpretation is too mechanistic. A government may be tempted to create a political business cycle, but not all governments will manipulate economic policies in the same way. Ultimately the economic methodology of the political business cycle models leads to the conclusion that democracy is inefficient. In chapter one it was argued that this conclusion is inappropriate: the conclusions and the normative recommendations follow from ideologically biased theories. Nevertheless, the opportunistic political mechanism is interesting, but it is only one of the factors that influence the policy choices of politicians. There are others, for example the ideological mechanism of partisan theory.

The models of the *partisan theory* assume that governments pursue ideological goals. Because political parties are guided by distinct ideologies, they have different economic objectives. Therefore, partisan governments employ different economic policies and affect the economy in a different manner. In general, a left-wing government is assumed to stimulate economic growth and to fight unemployment by higher public spending. A right-wing government is more concerned about inflation and employs deflationary policies. In this way a business cycle may be caused by alternating partisan governments. In chapter one it is explained how, in one way or another, the various models of the partisan theory, which incorporate the development of macroeconomic theory, are based on the Phillips curve. The central idea is that politics is about income distribution. It is argued that unemployment has negative distributional consequences for lower income groups, whereas inflation hurts the higher income groups. Partisan models are also mechanistic. They assume that governments automatically pursue ideological goals. However, the circumstances for governments to do so may not be to their advantage. There are reasons why it may be difficult for governments to pursue ideological or opportunistic goals.

One factor affecting the ability of governments to pursue political goals is the institutional context in which political decisions are made. It depends especially on the relationship of the government with the labour movement and the employers' organizations. For example, a left-wing government may be more successful if the labour movement facilitates left-wing economic policies. If wage demands are moderate, expansionary policies of left-wing governments may lead to less unemployment without running the risk of high inflation rates. A strong, centrally organized labour movement may succeed in moderating wage demands. Comparative political economy, or the politics of economics, is one scientific approach which studies these kinds of theories.

By discussing Scharpf's model, which is part of the politics of economics approach, an attempt was made to explain the policy choices of partisan governments in different political and economic situations. Scharpf's theory incorporates ideological and electoral objectives. Apart from these political objectives two additional factors are important, namely the international economic circumstances of the 1970s and 1980s and the behaviour of the labour unions. The interaction of the government with the labour movement determines part of the institutional structure in which the political actors play their role. By incorporating institutional interaction it is recognized that governments do not make economic policy all by themselves. Scharpf's model combines, to some extent, the institutional arguments of the politics of economics and the political mechanisms of the economics of politics.

The mechanisms of the political economic interaction models are interesting and warrant examination, in spite of the theoretical criticism on these kinds of models. They were therefore examined empirically in chapters two and three. The empirical tests on Dutch data led to some interesting results. In chapter two the partisan theory was subjected to an empirical examination. It is standard practice to use binary variables to distinguish between left and right-wing governments. In the Dutch situation of coalition governments such a binary division is not satisfactory. A few ideology variables were therefore constructed to capture Dutch partisan politics: (i) a variable which takes account of the division of power between the coalition partners; (ii) a variable, based on political science research, which takes account of the changing ideological preferences of the Dutch political parties; (iii) a variable taking the average value of the first two variables; and (iv) a simple binary variable to test the rational expectations variant of the partisan theory.

There were indications found of an ideological effect in the economic outcomes of the Netherlands. However, the results contradicted the expectations of the theoretical models. The partisan models assume, in simple terms, that left-wing governments seek to boost employment by Keynesian spending programmes which may result in inflationary pressures. In contrast, right-wing governments try to reduce inflation by taking austerity measures, possibly at the cost of higher unemployment. The results of the empirical exercises in chapter two did not point to a Phillips curve trade-off between unemployment and inflation in the Netherlands. There was also no extra economic growth or increased employment during centre-left governments, as the partisan theory expects to be the case. On the contrary, both inflation and unemployment appeared to be higher during centre-left governments than during centre-right ones. No evidence was found for the partisan theory with rational expectations. However, there were indications of a partisan effect on economic policy variables, in particular on total government expenditures and on social security spending. Taking account of unemployment, these spending variables were found to be higher during centre-left governments than during centre-right governments. The hypothesis that emerged was that in the Netherlands centre-left governments are more interested in direct income redistribution policies than in employment policies.

In chapter three the inadequacy of political business cycle theory for Dutch politics was discussed. Elections in the Netherlands do not take place with the same regularity as in, for example, the United States. Therefore, a number of election variables were constructed to take account of Dutch electoral politics. There was no political business cycle discernible in the Dutch macroeconomic outcomes. On the contrary, with respect to economic policy variables there were some indications of an opposite mechanism being at work. The significant increases or decreases of government spending seemed to have occurred in the beginning of or during a government's term of office and not in election years. In other words, important changes in government policies did not take place in election years. The conclusion was that Dutch coalition governments apparently do not choose policies in order to win elections, but want to be elected in order to be able to choose policies.

The objective of the description of political economic interaction in chapter four was to gain more insight into the actual influence ideological and opportunistic political goals have on Dutch political economic interaction. Chapter four provided further evidence for the hypothesis that in the Netherlands centre-left governments were indeed more interested in direct income redistribution policies than in employment policies, at least until the 1990s. The descriptive framework, based on Scharpf's model, suggested that there are two roads governments can follow: they can turn left or they can turn right. The results of their choices depend on international economic circumstances and the cooperative behaviour of the institutionalized political actors, namely the labour movement and the employers' organizations.

Centre-left governments, such as the Den Uyl government and, to a lesser extent, ˙Cabinet Lubbers/Kok, were assumed to employ income redistribution policies and Keynesian spending programmmes to stimulate employment. In terms of the theoretical framework these governments were expected to turn left. However, unless the labour movement succeeds in moderating wage demands, such measures run the risk of high inflation rates and high public finance deficits in a situation of stagflation. If wage demands are moderate, income redistribution policies, which are connected to wage developments, remain affordable and the risk of high inflation rates is reduced. Regarding the relation between the labour movement and the employers' organizations, an additional effect of wage moderation concerns the investment policies of employers: wage moderation may lead to more employment through more investments. The risk of the left-wing way is less private investments and a flight of capital abroad when production costs are rising.

Centre-right governments, like the ones led by Prime Minister Lubbers, were assumed to prefer to turn right. It was assumed that their priorities concern low inflation and low taxation. By aiming at lower production costs for the supply side of the economy these kinds of governments hope to stimulate investments and employment in the private sector. They consider the employers' organizations as their natural allies.

In relation to the analytical framework two government periods are of importance: the Den Uyl government in the 1970s and the two governments of Lubbers in the 1980s. The analytical framework explains why it was politically rational for the centre-left Den Uyl government to shift from Keynesian to monetarist policies. Due to changing international economic circumstances and the behaviour of the labour movement and of the employers, the Den Uyl government did not really choose to fight unemployment, but sticked to its income redistribution policies. In contrast, the governments of Lubbers in the 1980s turned right and chose to deal with inflation and public finance problems. Due to this policy and the wage moderation of the unions, private sector investment was stimulated. In accordance with Scharpf's model it was explained why it was only in the 1980s that wage demands were moderated and not in the 1970s during the Den Uyl government, as many corporatist theories assume. In sum, the success of policies, Keynesian or monetarist, is subject to international economic circumstances and the behaviour of the labour movement and the employers' organizations. The description of Dutch political interaction in chapter four provided an explanation for the failure of the partisan models to describe the political economic situation in the 1970s and 1980s.

For the 1990s, however, the model of Scharpf, emphasizing the different political ideas about macroeconomic policies, seems to have become less relevant. For example, specific tax policies and adjustments to the welfare system became more important for the Social Democrats in stimulating employment than Keynesian macroeconomic policies. Moreover, in the 1990s the main objective of the Social Democrats shifted from direct income redistribution policies to stimulating labour market participation. The consensus in Cabinet Kok between the PvdA and the VVD about this policy objective and the agreement with the social partners, supported by lowering the tax burden, to moderate wage demands explains the succes of the Dutch economy in recent years. It is clear that the interaction between the government and the employers' organizations is important for the Dutch model of policy-making, but this model is not an unchanging reality. The instability of it is illustrated by the fact that it is precisely Cabinet Kok that wanted to change the model by reducing the influence of the social partners in the process of economic policy-making. If economic circumstances deteriorate, the political relations may polarize again. It is not predictable what that would mean for the behaviour of the social partners and the social economic policies of the government.

Chapter four also showed that although governments react to economic circumstances and to the behaviour of other political actors, they also consider the electoral consequences of their policies. It was described how the shift from Keynesian to monetarist policies of Cabinet Den Uyl was electorally rational in terms of Scharpf's framework. Considering the electoral victory of the PvdA, voters apparently agreed with the explanation that due to international economic circumstances the government had to moderate its ideological policies. Moreover, the policy shift of the Den Uyl government did not involve drastic changes in income redistribution policies. Nevertheless, according to Scharpf's model the Christian Democrats should have won the elections and not the Social

Democrats, because the labour movement was not successful in moderating wage demands sufficiently. Although the policy shift of the Social Democratic government was rational, it should have led to an electoral victory only if the labour movement had responded by shifting from an agressive to a cooperative strategy.

The timing of the austerity measures of the Lubbers I and II governments and of the Lubbers/Kok government may have been influenced by electoral motives. These measures were indeed taken early in the government's term of office and not at the end. In election years these governments were careful about cutting public expenditures. In the case of the Lubbers/Kok government, the voters apparently had not forgotten the austerity measures regarding the disability benefits. However, the incomes policies at the end of Cabinet Kok's term of office does resemble the pattern of a political business cycle. It is obvious that electoral motives influence policy choices, but not as automatically as the models of the political business cycle assume. Chapter four described how policy choices were also influenced by economic developments, interaction with other political actors and partisan objectives. It is the combination of these factors that in the Netherlands determines the policies of coalition governments.

Ideology and opportunism play a role in the policy choices of governments, but there are also other factors. It is a combination of objectives, circumstances and coincidences that determines economic policies. This idea was part of this book through the recognition that neither mechanistic economic models (economics of politics) nor structural theories (politics of economics) can provide a complete answer to the questions it posed. To conclude, a few remarks are made about some factors that ought to be considered in theories of policy choices, but which were more or less neglected. The issue is that most theories of political economic interaction do not take account of changing realities.

In chapter two a few comments were made on the problem of changing preferences and how to cope with them. Acknowledging that preferences are not fixed, a variable based on the content of government programmes was constructed. This variable was aimed to take account of the developments in ideology on a left to right scale. By placing governments on this left to right scale, instead of using a simple binary variable, governments were not perceived to be either left- or right-wing governments, but it was acknowledged that election and government programmes change over time. Yet, by using this scale more fundamental shifts, brought about by policy reversals, were not taken into account. For example, political debates about macroeconomic policies were more important in the 1970s than in the 1990s. Furthermore, the political preferences of the Social Democrats seem to have changed. In the 1970s they prefered direct income redistribution measures, whereas they now attach more importance to policies which stimulate labour particiaption. If preferences change, political goals change. Such fundamental alterations were not incorporated in the economic models. It is obvious that the nature of political economic interaction changes as a consequence of changing preferences.

Although Scharpf's model analyses policy choices and possible shifts of political strategies, it does not explain these by shifting preferences of voter groups. Only the middle group of voters plays a pivotal role by shifting its votes to different parties under different economic circumstances. The reason why Scharpf's model cannot interpret electoral results, as the one for the Social Democrats in 1977, may be explained by the fact that this model does not analyse societal alterations and changing voter preferences (Kitschelt, 1994). According to Kitschelt the political strategies of political parties, especially the Social Democrats, have changed because of structural alterations in society. For example, the generally assumed class relations are no longer as relevant as they used to be. There is not that much difference between the political ideas of blue collar and white collar workers. More important are the differences in education, in gender or in profession. According to Kitschelt, Social Democratic political parties are no longer the representatives of the blue collar working class. There are new social economic groups and new interests that have to be taken into account. Such developments may explain the changing strategies of political parties in the 1980s and 1990s, especially those of the Social Democrats.

Nevertheless, Scharpf's model reflects an effort to take account of important policy changes. It aimed to explain why left-wing governments would shift their Keynesian to monetarist policies. The model stressed the importance of policy choices which governments may make depending on political and economic circumstances. In contrast, the mechanistic political economic interaction models did not take account of such developments at all. These theories have only been adapted to theoretical innovations in economic theory. For instance, by incorporating the principle of rational expectations the modern interaction models took account of novelties in economic theory. However, the political mechanisms and the political preferences remained the same. In other words, these models incorporated new theories, but did not incorporate changing realities. This confirms the proposition that mainstream economics has problems with studying changing realities, changing circumstances and changing preferences. In fact, there should be different models for different periods of time (see also Hood, 1994).

Changing preferences are related to, among other things, international developments. In the empirical exercises of the political business cycle models and the partisan models (chapters two and three) explicit account was taken of the international economic circumstances by incorporating variables such as growth of world trade, OECD-unemployment rates and OECD-inflation rates. By doing so it was acknowledged that it may be difficult for governments in a small and open country to affect the economy. In Scharpf's model the success of Keynesian policies depend, in a situation of stagflation, on the wage policies of the labour unions. In chapter four it was shown that international economic circumstances were part of the explanation of why the left-wing Den Uyl government abandoned left-wing economic policies. In other words, the empirical examinations in this book acknowledged that international economic relations can make national economic policies less effective. The question is whether changing international relations do not influence national politics more fundamentally. For instance, international economic developments, such as the oil crisis or the internationalization of economic relations (or the European process of integration, especially the Economic and Monetary Union (Snels, 1995b)), may affect national politics by changing the preferences of political actors and causing policies and institutions to adapt to such changes (see, for example, Milner and Keohane, 1996). If this is true, it is not sufficient to consider international economic variables, as was done in chapters two and three. It must then be considered whether international developments do not only determine to what extent political mechanisms affect the economy, but whether they also change the preferences of political actors and, eventually, the political mechanisms and the institutional structures.

The theories discussed in this book focus on short-term policy decisions. Institutional changes, in relation to policy reversals and changing voter preferences, were not the subject of this book. However, they are related to the policy choices of governments and may affect the political mechanisms. Hood (1994) discussed the political and economic theories of economic policy reversals. He enumerated a number of important factors, such as changing ideas on economic policy, shift of interests and social-political changes. Cohen (1995) posed the following question: if the partisan theory is correct, and governments follow ideological policies, how then is ideology formed and why does it alternate. This question was not discussed in this book, but an interesting theory about it, mentioned by both Hood and Cohen, is Hirschman's theory of the 'shifting involvements' (Hirschman, 1982, 1991). According to Hirschman there are long swings in politics and economics caused by the alternating dominance of conservative and progressive ideas. Since the 1980s conservative ideas have dominated the political economic debate. Whereas the 1960s were a period of growth and, therefore, a period of collectivist politics, the 1980s were a period of weak economic growth and individualist politics. In his theory of the shifting involvements Hirschman combines economic circumstances and dominant economic policies with social and psychological conditions. For some reason voters were disappointed with political achievements, got tired of collectivist politics, and wanted new political objectives.

The intention of these comments is not to say that political mechanisms and institutional structures are not important. However, international developments, societal changes, and significant ideological shifts are interrelated factors that may explain changing patterns of political economic interaction. This is the final conclusion of this book: to understand political economic interaction, political mechanisms are important as well as institutional structures, but to understand the working of political mechanisms in an institutional context, it is necessary to realize that institutional structures as well as political mechanisms are not fixed realities but change over time.

The question, finally, remains whether it is really possible to construct complete theories that can explain such complex developments. In this book reference was already made to Elster's distinction between mechanisms and theories or laws. As Elster noted, there is no law that says: if 'p', then sometimes 'q'. In this sense only mechanisms were discussed in this book. Such mechanisms may be helpful in understanding political economic relations, but it seems impossible to construct theories that have predictive power. In my opinion Hirschman's assertion put forward in an interview with Swedberg (1990: 164) is appropriate. With respect to the predictive power of social science theories he concluded: 'I think that we must be prepared to see social science fail... Were we ever to succeed, then mankind would have failed!'

List of Symbols

Macroeconomic variables (chapters 3 and 4)

RNI	real national income, annual mutation in %, 1952-1993 (CPB)
WORLD	annual mutation in % of weighted world trade, 1952-1993 (CPB)
DWORLD	WORLD(t)-WORLD(t-1)
UR	unemployment in % of dependent occupational population, 1952-1992 (CPB)
URNL	standard unemployment rate in % for the Netherlands, 1964-1993 (OECD)
UREC	standard unemployment rate in % for 12 countries of the European Community, 1964-1993 (OECD)
DUREC	UREC(t)-UREC(t-1)
EMPL	volume change in employment market sector, 1952-1992 (CPB)
INFLNL	yearly change consumer price index in % for the Netherlands, 1961-1993 (OECD)
INFLEC	idem for 12 countries of the European Community, 1962-1993 (OECD)

Economic policy variables (chapters 3 and 4)

GOVSP	government spending (*rijksuitgaven*), net in % net national income (market prices), 1952-1992 (CPB)
SOCSEC	social security spending in % national income, 1952-1991 (CBS)
GOVDEF	government deficit in % net national income (market prices), 1952-1993 (CPB (until 1970) and Miljoenennota)

Economic variables (chapter 5)

CTB	collective tax burden in % of gross domestic product (CPB)

CE	collective expenditures in % of gross domestic product (CPB)
MODAL	change in income of modal income category (CPB)
MINIMUMPLUS	change in income of income category on, or just above, minimum wage level (CPB)
MINIMUM	change in income of income category with minimum social security benefits (CPB)
LIS	labour income share (including self-employed) (CPB)

Ideology variables (chapter 3)

MINISTER	ideology variable - based on the variable of Van Dalen en Swank (1995a and b) - taking account of the number of left-wing and right-wing ministers in government
GOVERNM	ideology variable - based on the scale of Pennings and Keman (1993) - based on the content of government programmes (*regeerakkoorden*)
AVERAGE	ideology variable taking the average value of MINISTER and GOVERNM

Electoral variables (chapter 4)

A	all election years
A_L	all election years after centre-left government periods
A_R	all election years after centre-right government periods
B	years of and one year before elections
B_L	years of and one year before elections after centre-left government periods
B_R	years of and one year before elections after centre-right government periods
C	election years after more or less completed government periods
C_B	one year before election years after more or less completed government periods
C_A	one year after election years after more or less completed government periods
D	election years after more or less completed government periods (differs slightly from C in the timing of some cabinets)
D_L	election years after more or less completed centre-left government periods
D_R	election years after more or less completed centre-right government periods

List of Abbreviations

Political parties

ARP	Anti Revolutionary Party (Protestants) (*Anti Revolutionaire Partij*)
CDA	Christian Democratic Appeal (Christian Democrats) (*Christen Democratisch Appèl*)
CHU	Christian Historic Union (Protestants) (*Christelijk-Historische Unie*)
DS'70	Democratic Socialists (*Democratisch Socialisten 1970*)
D66	Democrats '66 (Social Liberals) (*Democraten 1966*)
KVP	Catholic People's Party (Catholics) (*Katholieke Volks Partij*)
PPR	Political Party Radicals (Left-wing Radicals) (*Politieke Partij Radicalen*)
PvdA	Labour Party (Social Democrats) (*Partij van de Arbeid*)
VVD	People's Party for Freedom and Democracy (Conservative Liberals) (*Volkspartij voor Vrijheid en Democratie*)

Labour organizations and employers' organizations

CNV	National Christian Federation of Labour Unions (*Christelijk Nationaal Vakverbond*)
FNV	Dutch Federation of Labour Unions (*Federatie Nederlandse Vakbeweging*)
MHP	Federation of Labour Unions for White Collar Workers (*Vakcentrale voor Middelbaar en Hoger Personeel*)
NKV	Dutch Catholic Federation of Labour Unions (*Nederlands Katholiek Vakverbond*)
NVV	Dutch Federation of Labour Unions (*Nederlands Verbond van Vakverenigingen*)
NCW	Christian Employers' Federation (*Nederlands Christelijk Werkgeversverbond*)
VNO	Federation of Dutch Enterprises (*Verbond van Nederlandse Ondernemingen*)

Other abbreviations

AOW	General Act on Old Age Benefits (*Algemene Ouderdomswet*)
CAO	Collective Labour Agreement (*Collectieve Arbeidsovereenkomst*)
CPB	Central Planning Bureau (*Centraal Planbureau*)
DNB	The Dutch Central Bank (*De Nederlandsche Bank*)
EC	European Community
OECD	Organization for Economic Cooperation and Development
SER	Social and Economic Council (*Sociaal-Economische Raad*)
WAO	Act on Disability Benefits (*Wet op de Arbeidsongeschikt-heidsverzekering*)

References

Albeda, W. (1987), 'Recent trends in collective bargaining in the Netherlands', in: J.P. Windmuller et al., *Collective bargaining in industrialized market economies: A reappraisal*, International Labour Office, Geneva.

Albeda, W. (1994), 'The Netherlands', in: A. Trebilcock et al., *Towards Social Dialogue: Tripartite cooperation in national economic and social policy-making*, International Labour Office, Geneva.

Albeda, W. and W.J. Dercksen (1994), *Arbeidsverhoudingen in Nederland*, Samson, Alphen aan den Rijn.

Alesina, A. (1987), 'Macroeconomic policy in a two-party system as a repeated game', *The Quarterly Journal of Economics*, August, 651-678.

Alesina, A. (1988), 'Macroeconomics and Politics', in: S. Fischer (ed.), *NBER Macroeconomics Annual 1988*, MIT Press, Cambridge.

Alesina, A. (1989), 'Politics and Business Cycles in Industrial Democracies', *Economic Policy*, 8, 55-87.

Alesina, A. (1995), 'Elections, party structure, and the economy', in: J.S. Banks and E.A. Hanushek (eds.), *Modern political economy. Old topics, new directions*, Cambridge University Press, Cambridge.

Alesina, A., G.D. Cohen and N. Roubini (1992), 'Macroeconomic Policy and Elections in OECD Democracies', *Economics and Politics*, 4(1), 1-30.

Alesina, A., G.D. Cohen and N. Roubini (1993), 'Electoral business cycle in industrial democracies', *European Journal of Political Economy*, 9, 1-23.

Alesina, A. and R. Perotti (1995), 'The Political Economy of Budget Deficits', *IMF Staff Papers*, 42(1), 1-31.

Alesina, A. and H. Rosenthal (1995), *Partisan politics, divided government, and the economy*, Cambridge University Press, Cambridge.

Alesina, A. and N. Roubini (1992), 'Political Cycles in OECD Economies', *Review of Economic Studies*, 59, 663-688.

Alesina, A. and J. Sachs (1988), 'Political Parties and the Business Cycle in the United States, 1948-1984', *Journal of Money, Credit, and Banking*, 20(1), 63-82.

Alt, J. (1980), 'Political Business Cycles in Britain', in: P. Whiteley (ed.), *Models of political economy*, Sage Publications, London.

Alt, J.E. (1985), 'Political Parties, World Demand, and Unemployment: Domestic and International Sources of Economic Activity', *The American*

Political Science Review, 79, 1016-1040.

Alt, J.E. and K.A. Chrystal (1983), *Political Economics*, University of California Press, Berkeley.

Alvarez, R.M., G. Garrett and P. Lange (1991), 'Government partisanship, labor organization, and macroeconomic performance', *The American Political Science Review*, 85, 539-556.

Amenta, E. (1993), 'The State of the Art in Welfare State Research on Social spending Efforts in Capitalist Democracies since 1960', *American Journal of Sociology*, 99(3), 750-763.

Armingeon, K. (1987), 'The compatability of economic, social, and political goals in economic policies. A comparative analysis of incomes policy developments in ten West European countries in the 1970s', in: H. Keman, H. Paloheimo, P.F. Whiteley (eds.), *Coping with the Economic Crisis, Alternative Responses to Economic Recession in Advanced Industrial Societies*, Sage Publications, London.

Arnhem, J.C.M. van, and G.J. Schotsman (1982), 'Do Parties Affect the Distribution of Income? The Case of Advanced Capitalist Democracies', in: F.G. Castles (ed.), *The Impact of Parties. Politics and Policies in Democratic Capitalist States*, Sage Publications, London.

Barro, R.J. and D.B. Gordon (1983), 'Rules, Discretion and Reputation in a model of Monetary Policy', *Journal of Monetary Economics*, 12, 101-121.

Barro, R.J. and D.B. Gordon (1985), 'A Positive Theory of Monetary Policy in a Natural Rate Model', *Journal of Political Economy*, 91(4), 589-611.

Barry, B. (1991), 'Does Democracy Cause Inflation? The Political Ideas of Some Economists', in: B. Barry, *Democracy and Power. Essays in Political Theory I*, Clarendon Press, Oxford.

Beck, N. (1982), 'Parties, Administrations, and American Macroeconomic Outcomes', *The American Political Science Review*, 76, 83-93.

Beck, N. (1987), 'Elections and the FED: Is there a Political Monetary Cycle?', *American Journal of Political Science*, 31, 194-216.

Beck, N. (1988), 'Politics and Monetary Policy', in: T.D. Willett (ed.), *Political Business Cycles. The political Economy of Money, Inflation, and Unemployment*, Duke University Press, Durham.

Beck, N., J. Katz, R.M. Alvarez, G. Garrett and P. Lange (1993), 'Government partisanship, labor organization, and macroeconomic performance: a corrigendum', *The American Political Science Review*, 87, 945-948.

Becker, G.S. (1983), 'A Theory of Competition among Pressure Groups for Political Influence', *The Quarterly Journal of Economics*, 98(3), 371-400.

Beus, J. de (1987), 'Inleiding. Wat is politieke economie?', in: J. de Beus and F. Vuijsje (eds.), *Politieke Economie*, Intermediar, Amsterdam.

Blais, A., D. Blake and S. Dion (1993), 'Do Parties Make a Difference? Parties and the Size of Government in Liberal Democracies', *American Journal of*

Political Science, 37(1), 40-62.

Boddy, R. and J. Crotty (1975), 'Class Conflict and Macro-Policy: The Political Business Cycle', *Review of Radical Political Economics*, 7(1), 1-19.

Borooah, V.K. and F. van der Ploeg (1983), *Political aspects of the economy*, Cambridge University Press, Cambridge.

Box, G.E.P. and G.M. Jenkins (1970), *Time Series Analysis, Forecasting and Control*, Holden -Day, San Francisco.

Box, G.E.P. and G.C. Tiao (1975), 'Intervention Analysis with Applications to Economic and Environmental Problems', *Journal of the American Statistical Association*, 70(349), 70-79.

Brennan, G. and J.M. Buchanan (1985), *The reason of rules. Constitutional political economy*, Cambridge University Press, Cambridge.

Brenner, Y.S. and N. Brenner-Golomb (1996), *A Theory of Full Employment*, Kluwer Academic Publishers, Dordrecht.

Bruno, M. and J. Sachs (1985), *Economics of Worldwide Stagflation*, Harvard University Press, Cambridge.

Bruyn, L.P.J. de, (1971), *Partij kiezen. Systematisch-vergelijkende analyse van de partijprograms voor de Tweede Kamerverkiezing 1971*, Samson Uitgeverij NV, Alphen aan den Rijn.

Buchanan, J.M. (1984), 'Politics without Romance: A Sketch of Positive Public Choice Theory and Its Normative Implications', in: J.M. Buchanan and R.D. Tollison (eds.), *The Theory of Public Choice II*, The University of Michigan Press, Ann Harbor.

Buchanan, J.M. and R.E. Wagner (1978), 'The political biases of Keynesian economics', in: J.M. Buchanan and R.E. Wagner (eds.), *Fiscal Responsibility in Constitutional Democracy*, Martinus Nijhoff, Leiden.

Byung Hee Soh (1986), 'National Elections and Policy Induced Business Cycles: A Historical perspective on the Literature', paper presented at the History of Economics Society Conference, Barnard College, New York, june 2-4.

Calmfors, L. and J. Driffill (1988), 'Centralization of wage bargaining', *Economic Policy*, April, 13-62.

Cameron, D.R. (1978), 'The Expansion of the Public Economy: A Comparative Analysis', *The American Political Science Review*, 72(2), 1243-1261.

Cameron, D.R. (1984), 'Social Democracy, Corporatism, Labour Quiescence and the Representation of Economic Interest in Advanced Capitalist Society', in: J.H. Goldthorpe (ed.), *Order and Conflict in Contemporary Capitalism*, Clarendon Press, Oxford.

Caporaso, J.A. and D.P. Levine (1992), *Theories of political economy*, Cambridge University Press, Cambridge.

Castles, F.G. (1982a), *The Impact of Parties. Politics and Policies in Democratic Capitalist States*, Sage Publications, London.

Castles, F.G. (1982b), 'The Impact of Parties on Public Expenditure', in: F.G.

Castles (ed.), *The Impact of Parties. Politics and Policies in Democratic Capitalist States*, Sage Publications, London.

Castles, F.G. (1987), 'Neocorporatism and the "happiness index", or what the trade unions get for their cooperation', *European Journal of Political Research*, 15, 381-393.

Castles, F. and P. Mair (1984), 'Left-Right Policy Scales: Some Expert Judgements', *European Journal of Politial Research*, 12, 83-88.

CBS (1989), *1899-1989. Negentig jaren statistiek in tijdreeksen*, SDU, Den Haag.

CBS (various issues), *Statistisch jaarboek*, SDU, Den Haag.

Chappell, H.W. and W.R. Keech (1986a), 'Policy Motivation and Party Differences in a Dynamic Spatial Model of Party Competition', *The American Political Science Review*, 80(3), 881-899.

Chappell, H.W. and W.R. Keech (1986b), 'Party Differences in Macroeconomic policies and Outcomes', *The American Economic Review, Papers and Proceedings*, 76(2), 71-74.

Clark, B. (1991), *Political Economy. A comparative approach*, Praeger, Westport.

Cohen, D. (1995), *The Misfortunes of Prosperity. An Introduction to Modern Political Economy*, The MIT Press, Cambridge.

CPB (various issues), *Centraal Economisch Plan* (CEP), Sdu Uitgevers, Den Haag.

CPB (1997), *Challenging Neighbours. Rethinking German and Dutch Economic Institutions*, Springer-Verlag, Berlin.

Crepaz, M.M.L. (1992), 'Corporatism in Decline? An Empirical Analysis of the Impact of Corporatism on Macroeconomic Performance and Industrial Disputes in 18 Industrialized Democracies', *Comparative Political Studies*, 25(2), 139-168.

Cukierman, A. and A.H. Meltzer (1986), 'A theory of Ambiguity, Credibility, and Inflation under Discretion and Asymmetric Information', *Econometrica*, 54(5), 1099-1128.

Czada, R. (1987), 'The impact of interest politics on flexible adjustment policies', in: H. Keman, H. Paloheimo, P.F. Whiteley (eds.), *Coping with the Economic Crisis. Alternative Responses to Economic Recession in Advanced Industrial Societies*, Sage Publications, London.

Dalen, H.P. van and O.H. Swank (1995a), 'Ideologie en opportunisme bij de overheidsuitgaven', *Economisch Statistische Berichten*, 19 April, 372-375.

Dalen, H.P. van and O.H. Swank (1995b), 'Government Spending Cycles: Ideological or Opportunistic', discussion paper, Tinbergen Instituut, Rotterdam.

Dalen, H.P. van and O.H. Swank (1996), 'Government spending cycles: Ideological or opportunistic?', *Public Choice*, 89, 183-200.

Demsetz, H. (1990), 'Amenity potential, indivisibilities, and political competition', in: J.E. Alt and K.A. Shepsle (eds.), *Perspectives on positive political economy*, Cambridge University Press, Cambridge.

Downs, A. (1957), *An Economic Theory of Democracy*, Harper & Row Publishers, New York.

Elster, J. (1989), *Nuts and Bolts for the Social Sciences*, Cambridge University Press, Cambridge.

Esping-Andersen, G. (1990), *The Three Worlds of Welfare Capitalism*, Princeton University Press, Princeton, New Jersey.

Esping-Andersen, G. and W. Korpi (1984), 'Social Policy as Class Politics in Post-War Capitalism: Scandinavia, Austria, and Germany', in: J.H. Goldthorpe (ed.), *Order and Conflict in Contemporary Capitalism*, Clarendon Press, Oxford.

Fortuyn, W.S.P. (1983), *Kerncijfers 1945-1983 van de sociaal-economische ontwikelling in Nederland, Expansie en Stagnatie*, Kluwer, Deventer.

Frey, B.S. (1978a), *Modern Political Economy*, Martin Robertson, Oxford.

Frey, B.S. (1978b), 'Politico-economic models and cycles', *Journal of Public Economics*, 9, 203-220.

Frey, B.S. and H.J. Ramser (1976), 'The Political Business Cycle: A Comment', *Review of Economic Studies*, 42, 553-555.

Frey, B.S. and F. Schneider (1978a), 'An empirical study of politico-economic interaction in the United States', *Review of Economics and Statistics*, 60, 174-183.

Frey, B.S. and F. Schneider (1978b), 'A politico-economic model of the United Kingdom', *The Economic Journal*, 88, 243-253.

Frey, B. and F. Schneider (1980), 'Popularity Functions: The Case of the US and West Germany', in P. Whiteley (ed.), *Models of Political Economy*, Sage Publications, London.

Friedman, M. (1976), 'Nobel Lecture: Inflation and Unemployment', *Journal of Political Economy*, 85(3), 451-472.

Garrett, G. and P. Lange (1986), 'Performance in a Hostile World: Economic Growth in Capitalist Democracies, 1974-1982', *World Politics*, no. 4, 517-545.

Gärtner, M. (1994), 'Democracy, elections, and macroeconomic policy: Two decades of progress', *European Journal of Political Economy*, 10, 85-109.

Gladdish, K. (1983), 'The 1982 Netherlands Election', *West European Politics*, 6(2), 277-280.

Gladdish, K. (1987), 'The Centre Holds: The 1986 Netherlands Election', *West European Politics*, 10(1), 115-119.

Gladdish, K. (1991), *Governing from the Centre. Politics and Policy-Making in the Netherlands*, Hurts & Company, London.

Glombowski, J. (1988), 'Interactie tussen een economische en een politieke cyclus', in: H.W. Plasmeijer (ed.), *De theoretische grondslagen van economisch beleid. Opstellen over Politieke Economie*, Wolters-Noordhof, Groningen.

Glombowski, J. (1989), 'Cyclical Interactions of Politics and Economics in an Abstract Capitalist Economy', Research Memorandum FEW 367, Tilburg University.

Glombowski, J. (1991), 'Modellen van interactie tussen economie en politiek', in: L. Golbach and W. Jansen (eds.), *Tussen Scylla en Charybdis. De veranderde gedaantes van de politieke economie*, Tilburg University Press, Tilburg.

Golden, D.G. and J.M. Poterba (1980), 'The Price of Popularity: The Political Business Cycle Reexamined', *American Journal of Political Science*, 24(4), 696-714.

Goodwin, R.M. (1967), 'A Growth Cycle', in: C.H. Feldstein (ed.), *Socialism, Capitalism and Economic Growth*, Cambridge University Press, Cambridge.

Grauwe, P. de (1985), 'Inflatie, werkloosheid en ideologie', *Economisch Statistische Berichten*, 9 October, 1003.

Grier, K.B. (1987), 'Presidential Elections and Federal Reserve Policy: An Empirical Test', *Southern Economic Journal*, 54, 475-486.

Grier, K.B. (1989), 'On the Existence of a Political Monetary Cycle', *American Journal of Political Science*, 33(2), 376-389.

Groenewegen, P. (1987), '"Political Economy" and "Economics"', in: J. Eatwell, M. Milgate and P. Newman (eds.), *The New Palgrave. The World of Economics*, The Macmillan Press, London.

Haynes, S.E. and J. A. Stone (1989), 'An Integrated Test for Electoral Cycles in the U.S. Economy', *The Review of Economics and Statistics*, 71(3), 426-434.

Haynes, S.E. and J. A. Stone (1990), 'Political Models of the Business Cycle Should Be Revived', *Economic Inquiry*, July, 442-465.

Havrilesky, T.M. (1987), 'A Partisanship Theory of Fiscal and Monetary Regimes', *Journal of Money, Credit, and Banking*, 19, 308-325.

Havrilensky, T. (1988), 'Two Monetary and Fiscal Policy Myths', in: T.D. Willett (ed.), *Political Business Cycles. The Political Economy of Money, Inflation, and Unemployment*, Duke University Press, Durham.

Hemerijck, A.C. (1992), *The historical contingencies of Dutch corporatism*, Balliol College, University of Oxford.

Hemerijck, A.C. (1994a), 'Hardnekkigheid van corporatistisch beleid in Nederland', *Beleid en Maatschappij*, 1-2, 23-47.

Hemerijck, A.C. (1994b), 'De politiek van de economie', *Beleid en Maatschappij*, 5, 229-245.

Hemerijck, A.C. and K. van Kersbergen (1997), 'A Miraculous Model? Explaining the New Politics of the Welfare State in the Netherlands', *Acta Politica*, 32(3), 258--280.

Hibbs, D.A. (1977a), 'Political Parties and Macroeconomic Policy', *The American Political Science Review*, 71, 1467-1487.

Hibbs, D.A. (1977b), 'On analyzing the effects of policy interventions: Box-Jenkins and Box-Tiao vs. structural equation models', in: D.R. Heise (ed.), *Sociological Methodology*, Jossey-Bass Publishers, San Francisco.

Hibbs, D.A. (1982), 'Economic Outcomes and Political Support for British Governments among Occupational Classes: A Dynamic Analysis', *The American Political Science Review*, 76, 259-279.

Hibbs, D.A. (1987a), *The Political Economy of Industrial Democracies*, Harvard University Press, Cambridge.

Hibbs, D.A. (1987b), *The American Political Economy. Macroeconomics and Electoral Politics*, Harvard University Press, Cambridge.

Hibbs, D.A. (1992), 'Partisan theory after fifteen years', *European Journal of Political Economy*, 8, 361-373.

Hibbs, D.A. (1994), 'The partisan model of macroeconomic cycles: more theory and evidence for the United States', *Economics and Politics*, 6(1), 1-23.

Hicks, A. (1988), 'Social Democratic Corportism and Economic Growth', *The Journal of Politics*, 50, 677-704.

Hicks, A. and J. Misra (1993), 'Political Resources and the Growth of Welfare in Affluent Capitalist Democracies, 1960-1982', *American Journal of Sociology*, 99(3), 668-710.

Hicks, A. and W.D. Patterson (1989), 'On the Robustness of the Left Corporatist Model of Economic Growth', *Journal of Politics*, 51(3), 662-675.

Hicks, A.M. and D.H. Swank (1992), 'Politics, Institutions, and Welfare Spending in Industrialized Democracies, 1960-82', *The American Political Science Review*, 86(3), 658-674.

Hirschman, A.O. (1982), *Shifting Involvements. Private Interest and Public Action*, Princeton University Press, Princeton.

Hirschman, A.O. (1991), *The Rhetoric of Reaction. Perversity, Futility, Jeopardy*, The Belknap Press of Harvard University Press, Cambridge.

Hoek, M.P. van der (1996), *Inkomensverdeling en economische orde*, Gouda Quint, Arnhem.

Hood, C. (1994), *Explaining economic policy reversals*, Open University Press, Buckingham.

Hoogerwerf, A. (1963), 'Sociaal-politieke strijdpunten: smeulend vuur', *Sociologische Gids*, 10(5), 249-263.

Hotelling, H. (1929), 'Stability in Competition', *Economic Journal*, 39, March, 1-57.

Huber, E. and J.D. Stephens (1993), 'Political Parties and Public Pensions. A Quantitative Analysis', *Acta Sociologica*, 36, 309-325.

Huber, E., C. Ragin and J.D. Stephens (1993), 'Social Democracy, Christian Democracy, Constitutional Structure, and the Welfare State', *American*

Journal of Sociology, 99(3), 711-749.

Irwin, G.A. and J.J.M. Holsteyn (1989), 'Decline of the Structured Model of Electoral Competition', in: H. Daalder and G.A. Irwin (eds.), *Politics in the Netherlands. How Much Change?*, Frank Cass, London.

Kalecki, M. (1971), 'Political aspects of full employment', in: M. Kalecki, *Selected essays on the dynamics of the capitalist economy 1933-1970*, Cambridge University Press, Cambridge, first published in 1943.

Katzenstein, P.J. (1983), 'The Small European States in the International Economy: Economic Dependence and Corporatist Politics', in: J.G. Ruggie (ed.), *The Antinomies of Independence, National Welfare and the International Division of Labor*, Columbia University Press, New York.

Katzenstein, P.J. (1985), *Small States in World Markets. Industrial Policy in Europe*, Cornell University Press, Ithaca.

Keech, W.R. (1995), *Economic politics. The costs of democracy*, Cambridge University Press, Cambridge.

Kenworthy, L. (1990), 'Labor Organization, Wage Restraint and Economic Performance', *Review of Radical Political Economics*, 22(4), 111-134.

Kersbergen, K. van (1995), *Social Capitalism. A study of Christian democracy and the welfare state*, Routledge, London.

Keizer, P. (1982), *Inflatie als politiek-economisch verschijnsel. Een theoretisch en empirisch onderzoek naar de invloed van ideologie en militantie op inflatie*, Stenfert Kroese, Leiden.

Keynes, J.M. (1973), *The General Theory of Employment, Interest and Money. The Collected Writings of John Maynard Keynes*, Macmillan, London, first published in 1936.

Kitschelt, H. (1994), *The Transformation of European Social Democracy*, Cambridge University Press, Cambridge.

Knoester, A. (1989), *Economische politiek in Nederland*, stenfert Kroese B.V., Leiden.

Koole, W. and G. Therborn (1987), 'De "Casablanca-solution" voorbij. De merkwaardige dood van het Keynesianisme en de relatieve verpaupering van Nederland', in: P. Fortuyn and S. Stuurman (eds.), *Socialisten in no nonsense tijd*, SUN, Nijmegen.

Korpi, W. (1983), *The democratic class struggle*, Routledge & Kegan Paul, London.

Korpi, W. (1991), 'Political and Economic Explanations for Unemployment: A Cross-National and Long-Term Analysis', *British Journal of Political Science*, 21, 315-348.

Kydland, F.E. and E.C. Prescott (1977), 'Rules Rather than Discretion: The Inconsistency of Optimal Plans', *Journal of Political Economy*, 85(3) 473-491.

Lange, P. and G. Garrett (1985), 'The Politics of Growth: Strategic Interaction and Economic Performance in the Advanced Industrial Democracies, 1974-1980', *Journal of Politics*, 47, 792-827.

Leamer, E. (1983), 'Let's take the Con out of Econometrics', *The American Economic Review*, 73, 31-43.

Lehmbruch, G. (1984), 'Concertation and the Structure of Corporatist Networks', in: J.H. Goldthorpe (ed.), *Order and Conflict in Contemporary Capitalism*, Clarendon Press, Oxford.

Lehmbruch, G. (1979), 'Consociational Democracy, Class Conflict, and the New Corporatism', in: P.C. Schmitter (ed.), *Trends Towards Corporatist Intermediation*, Sage Publications, Beverly Hills.

Lehner, F. (1987), 'Interest intermediation, institutional structures and public policy', in: H. Keman, H. Paloheimo, P.F. Whiteley (eds.), *Coping with the Economic Crisis. Alternative Responses to Economic Recession in Advanced Industrial Societies*, Sage Publications, London.

Lehner, F. and K. Schubert (1984), 'Party Government and the Political Control of Public Policy', European Journal of Political Research, 12, 131-146.

Lehning, P.B. (1989), 'Socialisten tussen plan en macht', in: J.W. de Beus, J.A.A. van Doorn and P.B. Lehning, *De ideologische driehoek. Nederlandse politiek in historisch perspectief*, Boom, Meppel.

Lijphart, A. (1989), 'From the Politics of Accommodation to Adversial Politics in the Netherlands: A Reassessment', in: H. Daalder and G.A. Irwin (eds.), *Politics in the Netherlands. How Much Change?*, Frank Cass, London.

Lindbeck, A. (1976), 'Stabilization Policy in Open Economies with Endogenous Politicians', *The American Economic Review. Papers and Proceedings*, 66, 1-19.

Lipschits, I. (1977), *Verkiezingsprogramma's 1977. Verkiezingen voor de Tweede Kamer der Staten-Generaal 1977*, Staatsuitgeverij, Den Haag.

Lipschits, I. (1981), *Verkiezingsprogramma's 1981. Verkiezingen voor de Tweede Kamer der Staten-Generaal 1981*, Staatsuitgeverij, Den Haag.

Lipschits, I. (1986), *Verkiezingsprogramma's 1986. Verkiezingen voor de Tweede Kamer der Staten-Generaal 21 mei 1986*, Staatsuitgeverij, Den Haag.

Lipschits, I. (1989), *Verkiezingsprogramma's 1989. Verkiezingen voor de Tweede Kamer der Staten-Generaal 6 september 1989*, SDU, Den Haag.

Locksley, G. (1980), 'The Political Business Cycle: Alternative Interpretations', in: P. Whiteley (ed.), *Models of political economy*, Sage Publications, London.

Lucas, R.J. (1973), 'Some International Evidence on Output-Inflation Tradeoffs', *The American Economic Review*, 63, 326-334.

MacRae, C.D. (1977), 'A Political Model of the Business Cycle', *Journal of Political Economy*, 85, 239-263.

Madsen, H.J. (1980), 'Electoral Outcomes and Macro-Economic Policies: The Scandinavian Cases', in: P. Whiteley (ed.), *Models of political economy*, Sage

Publications, London.

Maier, C.S. (1987), *In search of stability. Explorations in historical political economy*, Cambridge University Press, Cambridge.

McCallum, B.T. (1978), 'The Political Business Cycle: An Empirical Test', *Southern Economic Journal*, 44, 504-515.

Michels, A.B.M. (1993), *Nederlandse politieke partijen en hun kiezers (1970-1989)*, Faculteit Bestuurskunde, Universiteit Twente, Enschede.

Mierlo, H.J.G.A. van (1981), 'The 1981 Netherlands Election', *West European Politics*, 4(3), 297-301.

Miliband, R. (1991), *Divided Societies. Class Struggle in Contemporary Capitalism*, Oxford University Press, Oxford.

Miljoenennota (various issues), Sdu Uitgeverij Plantaanstraat, Den Haag.

Milner, H.V. and R.O. Keohane (1996), Internationalization and Domestic Politics: An Introduction', in: R.O. Keohane and H.V. Milner (eds.), *Internationalization and Domestic Politics*, Cambridge University Press, Cambridge.

Mueller, D.C. (1989), *Public Choice II. A revised edition of Public Choice*, Cambridge University Press, Cambridge.

Nannestad, P. and M. Paldam (1994), 'The VP-function: A survey of the literature on vote and popularity functions after 25 years', *Public Choice*, 79, 213-245.

Niskanen, W.D. (1971), *Bureaucracy and Representative Government*, Aldine-Atherton, Chicago.

Nordhaus, W.D. (1975), 'The Political Business Cycle', *Review of Economic Studies*, 42, 169-190.

Nordhaus, W.D. (1989), 'Alternative Approaches to the Political Business Cycle', *Brookings Papers on Economic Activity*, 2, 1-68.

OECD (1994), *International Statistic Yearbook*, Data Service & Information GMBH (CD-ROM), Gesellschaft für Wirtschaftsanalyse und -Prognose, Rheinberg.

OECD (1998), *OECD economic surveys, 1997-1998, Netherlands*, OECD, Paris.

Olson, M. (1982), *The rise and decline of nations. Economic Growth, Stagflation, and Social Rigidities*, Yale University Press, New Haven.

Panitch, L. (1980), 'Recent Theorizations of Corporatism: Reflections on a Growth Industry', British Journal of Sociology, 31, 161-187.

Pennings, P. and J.E. Keman (1993), '"Links" en "rechts" in de Nederlandse politiek', *Documentatiecentrum Nederlandse politieke partijen, Jaarboek 1993*, Groningen.

Persson, T. and G. Tabellini (1990), *Macroeconomic Policy, Credibility and Politics*, Harwood Academic Publishers, Chur.

Pindyck, R.S. and D.L. Rubinfeld (1991), *Econometric Models and Economic Forecasts. Third edition*, McGraw-Hill, inc., New York.

Przeworski, A. (1990), *The State and the Economy under Capitalism*, Harwood Academic Publishers, Chur.

Renaud, P.S.A. (1989), *Applied Political Economic Modelling*, Springer-Verlag, Berlin.

Renaud, P. S.A. and F.A.A.M. van Winden (1987), 'On the importance of elections and ideology for government policy in a multi-party system', in: M.J. Holler (ed.), *The Logic of Multiparty Systems*, Kluwer Academic Publishers, Dordrecht.

Reynaerts, W.H.J. and A.G. Nagelkerke (1986), *Arbeidsverhoudingen, theorie en praktijk, deel 1, tweede druk*, Stenfert Kroese B.V., Leiden.

Riel, B. van (1995), *Unemployment Divergence and Coordinated Systems of Industral Relations*, Peter Lang, Frankfurt am Main.

Robbins, L. (1976), *Political Economy: Past and Present*, The MacMillan Press LTD, London.

Rogoff, K. (1990), 'Equilibrium Political Budget Cycles', *The American Economic Review*, 80, 21-36.

Rogoff, K. and Sibert (1988), 'Elections and Macroeconomic Policy Cycles', *Review of Economic Studies*, LV, 1-16.

Rose, R. (1980), *Do parties make a difference?*, Macmillan Press, London.

Sargent, T.J. and N. Wallace (1975), '"Rational" Expectations, the Optimal Monetary Instrument, and the Optimal Money Suypply Rule', *Journal of Political Economy*, 83(2), 341-255.

Scharpf, F.W. (1984), 'Economic and Institutional Constraints of Full-Umployment Strategies: Sweden, Austria, and Wesren Germany, 1973-1982', in: J.H. Goldthorpe (ed.), *Order and Conflict in Contemporary Capitalism*, Clarendon Press, Oxford.

Scharpf, F.W. (1987), 'A Game-Theoretical Interpretation of Inflation and Unemployment in Western Europe', *Journal of Public Policy*, 7(3), 227-257.

Scharpf, F.W. (1991), *Crisis and Choice in European Social Democracy*, Cornell University Press, Ithaca.

Schmidt, M.G. (1982), 'The Role of the Parties in Shaping Macroeconomic Policy', in: F.G. Castles (ed.), *The Impact of Parties. Politics and Policies in Democratic Capitalist States*, Sage Publications, London.

Schmitter, P.C. (1979), 'Still the Century of Corporatism?', in: P.C. Schmitter (ed.), *Trends Towards Corporatist Intermediation*, Sage Publications, Beverly Hills.

Schmitter, P.C. (1981), 'Interest intermediation and regime governability in contemporary Western Europe and North America', in: S.D. Berger (ed.), *Organizing interests in Western Europe: pluralism, corporatism, and the transformation of politics*, Cambridge University Press, Cambridge.

Schultz, K.A. (1995), 'The Politics of the Political Business Cycle', *British Journal of Political Science*, 25, 79-99.

Schumpeter, J.A. (1976), *Capitalism, Socialism and Democracy*, George Allen & Unwin Publishers, London, first published in 1943.

Sijben, J.J. (1979), *Rationele verwachtingen en de monetaire politiek*, Stenfert Kroese, Leiden.

Snels, B. (1995a), '"Linkse" en "rechtse" politiek in de Nederlandse economie', *Beleid en Maatschappij*, 6, 342-354.

Snels, B. (1995b), 'Models of Politics and Economics: National Economic Policy in an Integrating Europe', paper presented at 53rd annual meeting of the Association for Social Economics, January 8th, 1995, Washington DC.

Stevens, R.J.J., L.J. Giebels and P.F. Maas (1994), *De formatiedagboeken van Beel 1945-1973, handboek voor formateurs*, Sdu uitgeverij, 's-Gravenhage.

Swaan, A. de (1982), 'The Netherlands: Coalitions in a Segmented Polity', in E.C. Browne and J. Dreijmanis, *Government Coalitions in Western Democracies*, Longman, New york.

Swedberg, R. (1990), *Economics and Sociology. Redefining their boundaries: conversations with economists and sociologists*, Princeton University Press, Princeton.

Thelen, k. and S. Steinmo (1992), 'Historical institutionalism in comparative politics', in: S. Steinmo, K. Thelen and F. Longstreth (eds.), *Structuring politics*, Cambridge University Press, Cambridge.

Therborn, G. (1986), *Why Some Peoples Are More Unemployed Than Others. The Strange Paradox Of Growth And Unemployment*, Verso, London.

Therborn, G. (1989), '"Pillarization" and "Popular Movements". Two Variants of Welfare State Capitalism: the Netherlands and Sweden', in: F.G. Castles (ed.), *The Comparative History of Publlic Policy*, Polity Press, Cambridge.

Tinbergen, J. (1952), *On the Theory of Economic Policy*, North-Holland, Amsterdam.

Tinbergen, J. (1970), 'De ontwikkeling van de plangedachte', in: Centraal Planbureau, *25 jaar Centraal Planbureau*, monografie no. 12, Staatsuitgeverij, Den Haag.

Toirkens, J. (1988), *Schijn en werkelijkheid van het bezuinigingsbeleid 1975-1986*, Kluwer, Deventer.

Traxler, F. (1990), 'Political Exchange, Collective Action and Interest Governance. Towards a Theory of the Genesis of Industrial Relations and Corporatism', in: B. Marin (ed.), *Governance and Generalized Exchange. Self-Organizing Policy Networks in Action*, Campus/Westview, Frankfurt am Main.

Tromp, B. (1989), 'Party Strategies and System Change in the Netherlands', *West European Politics*, 12(4), 82-97.

Tufte, E.R. (1978), *Political Control of the Economy*, Princeton University Press, Princeton, New Jersey.

Uyl, J.M. den (1978), 'De smalle marge van democratische politiek', in: idem,

Inzicht en uitzicht. Opstellen over economie en politiek, Uitgeverij Bert Bakker, Amsterdam.

Veldhoven, B.C.J. van (1988), *The Endogenization of Government Behaviour in Macroeconomic Models*, Offsetdrukkerij Kanters B.V., Alblasserdam.

Visser, J. (1990), 'Continuity and Change in Dutch Industrial Relations', in: G. Baglioni and C. Crouch (eds.), *European Industrial Relations. The Challenge of Flexibility*, SAGE Publications, London.

Visser, J. (1992), 'The Netherlands: The End of an Era and the End of a System', in: A. Ferner and R. Hyman (eds.), *Industrial Relations in the New Europe*, Blackwell, Oxford.

Visser, J. and A. Hemerijck (1997), *'A Dutch Miracle'. Job Growth, Welfare Reform and Corporatism in the Netherlands*, Amsterdam University Press, Amsterdam.

Visser, W. and R. Wijnhoven (1989), *Baanbrekende politiek. De achterkant van de massale werkloosheid*, Kok Agora, Kampen.

Visser, W. and R. Wijnhoven (1990), 'Politics do matter, but does unemployment? Party strategies, ideological discourse and enduring mass unemployment', *European Journal of Political Research*, 18, 71-96.

Waarden, F. van (1997), 'Institutions of Socio-Economic Coordination: A European Style?', in: Ministry of Social Affairs and Employment, *Social Policy and Economic Performance*, Den Haag.

Whiteley, P. (1986), *Political Control of the Macroeconomy. The Political Economy of Public Policy Making*, Sage, London.

Wiardi Beckman Stichting (1963), *Om de kwaliteit van het bestaan. I. De besteding van de groei van het nationaal inkomen*, N.V. De Arbeiderspers, Amsterdam.

Wijck, P. van (1989), 'Inkomensbeleid in een representatieve democratie', *Mens en Maatschappij*, 64(2), 142-165.

Wijck, P. van (1990), 'Inkomensherverdeling: een verklaring vanuit de economische theorie van het politieke proces', *Maandschrift Economie*, 54, 294-307.

Wijck, P. van (1991a), *Inkomensverdelingsbeleid in Nederland. Over individuele voorkeuren en distributieve effecten*, Thesis/Tinbergen Instituut, Amsterdam.

Wijck, P. van (1991b), 'Ideologie en economisch beleid', *Economisch Statistische Berichten*, 20 March, 305-308.

Wijck, P. van (1997), 'Internationale en binnenlands-politieke invloeden op de economische groei in Nederland', *Maandschrift Economie*, 61, 65-78.

Wijck, P. van, and W. Arts (1991), 'The Dynamics of Income Inequality in a Representative Democracy, The Case of the Netherlands', *Rationality and Society*, 3(3), 317-342.

Wilensky, H.L. (1976), *The "new corporatism". Centralization and the welfare state*, Sage, London.

Wilensky, H.L. (1984), 'Leftism, Catholocicism, and Democratic Corporatism: The Role of Political Parties in Recent Welfare Sate Development', in: P. Flora and A.J. Heidenheimer (eds.), *The Development of Welfare States in Europe and America*, Transaction Books, New Brunswick, first printing 1981.

Wilke, M. (1991a), *Corporatism and the Stability of Capitalist Democracies*, Peter Lang, Frankfurt am Main.

Wilke, M. (1991b), 'Veranderde gedaantes van de politieke economie', in: L. Golbach and W. Jansen (eds.), *Tussen Scylla en Charybdis. De veranderde gedaantes van de politieke economie*, Tilburg University Press, Tilburg.

Winden, F.A.A.M van (1983), *On the Interaction between State and Private Sector*, North-Holland, Amsterdam.

Windmuller, J.P., C. de Galan and A.F. van Zweeden (1983), *Arbeidsverhoudingen in Nederland*, Uitgeverij Het Spectrum, Utrecht.

Woldendorp, J. (1993), 'Christen-democratie en neo-corporatisme in Nederland. Het CDA en het maatschappelijk middenveld', in: K. van Kersbergen, P. Lucardie, H. ten Napel (eds.), *Geloven in macht. De christen-democratie in Nederland*, Het Spinhuis, Amsterdam.

Woldendorp, J.J. (1995), 'Neo-corporatism as a strategy for conflict regulation in the Netherlands (1970-1990)', *Acta Politica*, 30(2), 121-151.

Wolinetz, S.B. (1989), 'Socio-economic Bargaining in the Netherlands: Redefining the Post-war Policy Coalition', in: H. Daalder and G.A. Irwin (eds.), *Politics in the Netherlands. How Much Change?*, Frank Cass, London.

Wolinetz, S.B. (1990a), 'The Dutch Election of 1989: Return to the Centre-Left', *West European Politics*, 13(2), 280-286.

Wolinetz, S.B. (1990b), 'A quarter century of Dutch politics: a changing political system or le plus que change..?', *Acta Politica*, 4, 403-431.

For Product Safety Concerns and Information please contact our EU
representative GPSR@taylorandfrancis.com Taylor & Francis Verlag GmbH,
Kaufingerstraße 24, 80331 München, Germany

Printed and bound by CPI Group (UK) Ltd, Croydon, CR0 4YY
08/05/2025
01864412-0004